What Others Say About *PUBLICITY WRITING FOR TELEVISION & FILM* by Rolf Gompertz

"I'm delighted that such a book is finally available for emerging and veteran publicists alike. The Publicists Guild of America has for some years campaigned for the creation of educational programs to help elevate the standards of the profession. This book, which offers the most succinct and clear to follow 'how to' information on the subject, is sure to become a vital teaching tool. Anyone following the author's strategies can learn to write effective releases and press kits for television shows and films."

HENRI BOLLINGER, President
The Publicists Guild of America

"This handbook is the one comprehensive text for publicity rookies and veterans alike. It is for the student, too, and I am recommending it in my USC Entertainment Public Relations classes."

HANK RIEGER, Editor/Publisher
EMMY magazine

"This book is a great resource. It contains everything you've ever wanted to know about writing a first-class publicity campaign."

MICHAEL O'HARA, Writer/Producer
O'Hara/Horowitz Productions, formerly
Vice President, Media Relations, NBC

"The author has provided a superb book for those planning a career in television or film publicity. With its easily understood text and abundant examples drawn from actual news releases, pitch letters, and press kits, this book is a must for anyone considering a career in entertainment publicity. I find it truly satisfying to see a well-conceived, abundantly-illustrated handbook that clearly defines the writing requirements and procedures that both the author and I had to learn without the benefit of such a guide."

EDWARD S. CRANE
EDitorial Ink Publicity Writing Service
formerly Head writer, Universal Pictures and
Warner Bros. Inc.

"Rolf Gompertz is one of the true experts in the field of publicity writing. I have used his skills over several years on numerous projects. This book is a useful and informative compilation of the author's demonstrated talents in this area. It would be helpful for not only the beginning publicity writer but also the more seasoned professional who wants to perfect his or her skills."

BARBARA GOEN
Vice President, Public Information, KCET
Public Television for Southern & Central Calif.

"There's no doubt that college students, as well as those entering the practical business of entertainment publicity, will find this an invaluable guide. Frankly, there are quite a few people who are well *beyond* entry-level who could profit from studying the excellent examples presented here."

CAROL STEVENS
Carol Stevens & Associates Public Relations

"This is a vital workbook for neophyte publicists and industry veterans alike. Not only does the author explain the various types of writing that are an intrinsic part of public relations campaigns in both television and film, but he supplies a treasure-trove of actual writing samples and a snappy running commentary on their salient elements -- good or bad. Another thoughtful discourse from one of our top public relations professionals."

STEVEN JAY RUBIN, Author, "Reel Exposure:
How Publicize and Promote Today's
Motion Pictures" (Broadway Press 1992)

PUBLICITY WRITING

FOR

TELEVISION & FILM

A How-To Handbook

by ROLF GOMPERTZ

The Word Doctor Publications
P.O. Box 9761
No. Hollywood, CA 91609-1761
Phone: (818) 980-3576
Fax: (818) 985-7922

Other books by Rolf Gompertz:
PUBLICITY ADVICE & HOW-TO HANDBOOK (The Word Doctor Publications, 1988, revised, 1990, 1992) For details, please see last page of this book.

Please address inquiries or suggestions to:

Rolf Gompertz, Author/Publisher
The Word Doctor Publications
P.O. Box 9761
No. Hollywood, CA 91609-1761
Phone no.: (818) 980-3576
FAX: (818) 985-7922

Printed in the United States of America

CONTENTS

ACKNOWLEDGMENTS

I would like to thank Dr. Barry Bortnick of the Humanities & Social Sciences Department at UCLA Extension for inviting me to develop a course on Publicity Writing for Television and Film in 1991, in association with the Publicists Guild of America/IATSE 818. This book came about to meet the needs of that course and of TV and film publicists. I would also like to acknowledge veteran Hollywood publicist Ed Crane, who helped pioneer the course with me, Ed teaching film publicity writing, while I teach TV publicity writing.

I would like to thank the following for the use of their publicity materials. Copyrights to these materials, of course, remain with these companies:

ABC
CBS
HBO
KCET
NBC
PBS
Academy of Television Arts & Sciences
Baker, Winokur, Ryder Public Relations
Bob Palmer Public Relations
The Brokaw Company
Owen Comora Associates
Devillier Communications
Richard Grant & Associates
Hanna-Barbera Productions, Inc.
Hallmark Cards/Television Programming
Ketchum Public Relations
King World
The Lippin Group
Mahoney Communications, Inc.
National Geographic Society/Television Division
Orion Television Entertainment
Paramount Pictures/Network Television Division
Carol Stevens & Associates Public Relations
Stone/Hallinan Associates, Inc.
Warner Bros. Inc.
Weissman/Angellotti

1

ABOUT THIS BOOK

Δ **This is a book about writing**. It is a book about professional writing, particularly about publicity writing, for television and film.

Δ **Writing is an art for which one has to have an aptitude**. It requires a feeling for language, an ear for the sound of words, a sense of rhythm for the structure and flow of sentences.

Δ **Given that, writing is a skill that can be taught and learned.**

This book will presume two things: 1) That the reader will have an aptitude for writing -- which cannot be taught, and 2) that he or she will have a knowledge of English grammar and composition -- which should have been learned in high school or college.

A prior understanding of journalistic writing or public relations writing is an advantage, but it is not essential, since I will explain the basics and offer examples relating to television and film publicity.
    This handbook is being written for a number of reasons:
    1) To provide explanations and examples of publicity writing in TV and film for individuals who want to get into this field but who do not have access to such information;
    2) To provide an on-the-job training manual and reference book for entertainment industry publicists;
    3) To provide agencies, studios, production companies, TV stations, and networks with resource material that will save time and money in training full-time, part-time, and temporary publicists;
    4) To provide an instructional text for colleges and universities.

Δ **Writing is rewriting**. I offer that as a definition of professional writing -- of any kind. Get used to this idea right away. Don't fight it. The first thing you put down on paper -- or on your computer -- will not be the final thing. Even after years of professional writing, you will still keep rewriting. It is inherent in the process. It is what separates good craftsmen from bad craftsmen, good writers from bad writers -- pros from non-pros.

Δ **Writing is sculpting with words**. Think of yourself as a sculptor working with clay. First you shape the mass of clay, giving it form. Then you refine it, adding something here, taking something away there. That's what we do with words, too. Whether it's a book, a play, a short story, a screenplay, a TV

1

drama, or a publicity release, we first work on the form and then we work on the words.

Take a news release. It will take several drafts before it says what you want it to say, in the order in which you want to say it. Paragraphs and even sentences will need switching. Even then, a sentence may not read correctly and will need changing. When the paragraphs and sentences are finally all in place, you will find a word here and there which isn't right or which could be replaced with a better word. Writing is re-writing.

Do not turn your writing over to anyone until you have completed the re-writing process to your fullest satisfaction. The reason is simple: your reputation as a writer is at stake every time. If you turn in a badly written draft for someone else to read, you will quickly be pegged as a sloppy writer whose work is not dependable. Once you have that label, it becomes hard, if not impossible, to shake.

So, who else gets to approve your copy? That depends on the organization and the nature of the release. Let's say you're working for a network, for instance. You have prepared a release announcing a new TV series. Your copy may go to the publicity manager you work for; then to the head of your department; then to the programming executive in charge of the new series. It could even go to the head of the network. After they've made their comments or changes, the release may go to the studio or production company that will be producing the series. It may go to a studio head, an executive producer, a producer, a star, and even the publicists representing these various entities. Be prepared to have your release run this gauntlet. It is a normal part of the process.

Not every release goes this route. But there is always someone who will need to see your release. Your client has a right to see what you're sending to the media. If you're writing a biography, for instance, the subject of the biography has a right to see what you have written. Don't be surprised if everyone's asked to get into the act, including husbands, wives, and significant-others. It comes with the territory.

I have the following sign above my desk, author unknown:

> **The strongest drive is not
> love or hate.
> It is one person's need to
> change another's copy.**

The word "change" is crossed out, and several supposedly "better" words are scribbled around it: revamp, rework, amend, improve, rewrite. They, too, are crossed out, and the word "change" is re-inserted.

Thereby hangs a tale! What's the big deal about writing? Everyone's a critic! Some people will drive you crazy. They'll ask you to change something, and then they'll ask you to change it again. Worse, they won't be able to tell you how they want something changed, but they'll want you to change it, and you try to guess what they mean from their inarticulate mumblings and flailing body language. But before we writers circle the wagons, a word of caution is in order. Our job is to take the information which we have been given and to express it professionally. The more experience we have, the better we get at doing this. Most of the time we hit the bull's eye, or come close to it. However, we must guard against professional arrogance. The fact that we are writers does not make us automatically right! The people who give us the information have lived with the project much longer than we have. They have thought about it and talked about it for days, weeks, months and even years. They can provide us with words, phrases and ideas that will actually improve the final copy. This, too, is a valuable part of the fine-tuning process.

However, there are times when you must resist and take a stand. One is when the requested change would be contrary to journalistic style. The other is when you believe that you have a good, legitimate reason for the way you have stated something, which the other person may not have realized or understood, or that the change you are being asked to make could even be detrimental to the client's interest. Make your case, but be diplomatic. However, don't make an issue out of everything. Just take a stand on essentials. Otherwise, people will think you're combative on everything. You will lose credibility -- and, eventually, you'll wear out your welcome. There are different ways of writing things. If it's not a serious matter, go with the flow.

If your copy is well written, there usually aren't that many major changes, even though your document must pass through a number of checkpoints. But there are times when the rewrites don't quit. Just remember: this is the process. If you are a good, veteran writer, don't take it personally. If you're a beginning publicity writer, learn from it.

Δ **Everything in life has structure, everything in nature has form**: a tree, a flower, a chair, a table, a house. The same is true of publicity writing. Here are some of its forms: a news release, biography, feature story, format story, storyline, pitch letter, fact sheet, caption, credit sheet. You can tell immediately what something is by looking at its form, its structure. If your release is not written -- that is, structured -- correctly, it will not serve its function and get the results you wish to obtain. It will be thrown away -- a waste of time and money. However, just as there are many types of trees and flowers and chairs and tables and houses, so there are variations within publicity forms.

Δ **This book is designed to show you 1) the difference between the forms and 2) the variations within these forms.** The forms vary from network to network, studio to studio, production company to production company, agency to agency. A professional writer not only must be a good writer but also a flexible writer. A professional writer must be able to analyze an organization's publicity style and structure at a glance and write accordingly. Sometimes a style change is instituted within your own company and you must accommodate yourself to the changes. More often, you will notice stylistic and structural differences as you move from one company to another. A final word of caution: when you change jobs, the last thing your new boss wants to hear from you is, "That's not how we did it at...." Unless you are in charge or are asked to introduce changes, remember, "When in Rome...."

So, why make such a big deal about writing? There's more to being a publicist than that, isn't there? Yes and no.

Δ **Writing is basic.** A publicist must know how to write. Even when you become management, you must be able to supervise and evaluate other people's writing. One of the greatest complaints we hear from PR department heads and PR agency owners is that people don't know how to write. Most places now ask PR job applicants to take a written test, demonstrating that they can write. Furthermore, companies cannot afford the luxury of large staffs any more, where people who do not know how to write are given other kinds of work. The person with the most skills, including the ability to write, has the best chance of surviving company and departmental cutbacks. The more versatile you are, the more valuable you are.

Finally, let me say, there's a limit to what you can learn from reading about writing. Take a journalism or PR writing course. If you're lucky, you will find courses in TV and film publicity writing. **Ultimately, the only way you learn to write is by writing and writing and writing and writing...and more writing.**

Δ **PRESS MATERIALS:** Each chapter provides examples of topics under discussion. These press materials may be found, usually in the order in which they are being discussed, at the end of each chapter. For easy reference, they are identified in **bold-face** by name at the beginning of the paragraph in which they are discussed.

2

ANNOUNCEMENT STORIES
&
FOLLOW-UP STORIES

There are different types of news releases in TV and film publicity writing involving corporate or programming matters. Each has its peculiarities, which we will discuss, yet they all have one thing in common: the basic journalistic news structure.

Δ **The five Ws.** We're talking about the five Ws and the inverted pyramid style. As every journalism student knows, the first paragraph of your news story must be able to answer five questions: Who, What, When, Where, and Why (or, How). These are the five Ws. If your first paragraph does not answer those questions, you must work on it until it does.

Δ **The inverted pyramid.** The inverted pyramid style of writing means that you go from most important to least important, with your first paragraph containing the most important information. It must contain the essentials of your story. Subsequent paragraphs may provide further details. You must organize your information so that each paragraph becomes a less important paragraph.

The reason for this is that editors will cut your story from the bottom up, if they must shorten it because of l) limited space or 2) limited news value.

Δ **Facts & feelings.** Finally, you must exercise care in your choice of words. A news release must contain facts. Be careful with adjectives and descriptions. The tone of a news release must be one of *understatement.* If you want to inject feelings, emotions, opinion, commentary, there's just one permissible way of doing that: quote somebody. If the person wants to indulge in superlatives, and wax exuberant, fine. Just don't you do it. (It's OK to prepare such quotes for your client, but the quotes must be approved by your client before you may use them.)

Δ **Length.** The length of a news release should be determined by how much newsworthy information you have to report. If you have a lot, go a page-and-a-half or two pages. If you don't have a lot, go three or four paragraphs. Can you ever go more than two pages? Yes, if it's really an important story and there's a lot to report -- it may not get used in full, in fact, chances are it won't get used in full, but the additional information may provide the editor with background material for a full understanding of the story now or later.

The shorter the release the better, but if it's an important story don't sell yourself short.

Here's a way you can train yourself in writing news releases. After you have gathered all your information, give each piece of information a value, from #1 to #5 , #1 being highest. Giving it a "1" means the information is absolutely essential (it is one of the five Ws) and must go into the first paragraph. Numbers 2, 3, 4, 5 then become paragraphs 2, 3, 4, 5. That's an easy way of learning the inverted pyramid style of news writing (for a longer news release, increase the numbers).

Weighing the relative value of information is a matter of educated guessing, psychology, and news instinct. You can't put it on a scientific basis.

Δ **Structure.** I cannot stress enough how important it is to structure your news release properly and to work on that first paragraph until it is polished to perfection. Let me give you two examples.

The first release involved a client, Nancy Zala, an actress, writer, and director, who had financed and produced her own feature film. Having completed production, she needed to bring this project to the attention of the entertainment industry to create interest, especially among distributors. So we needed to produce a news release.

The point is that your first draft is seldom, if ever, your final draft. *Remember, writing is rewriting.* And when you write, don't just look at the words, and read the words, also, listen to the words. Do they sound right together? Do they flow?

The reason the first draft is not your final draft is because you are dealing with a lot of new information which you must pound into shape. It must be structured properly and the meaning must be made crystal clear.

Following was the first draft of this particular news release.

CONTACT:
Rolf Gompertz
(818) 980-3576

'ROUND NUMBERS' COMPLETES PRINCIPAL PHOTOGRAPHY

Principal photography has been completed on "Round Numbers," a new feature film written and directed by Nancy Zala and produced by Allan Mann.

The black comedy began production in Los Angeles in October 1990 and is based upon Zala's play, "Women Who Eat Too Much."

Kate Mulgrew stars as Judith, a middle-aged woman whose marriage to "Big Al Schweitzer The Muffler King" (Marty Ingels) is based more on business than pleasure. Suspecting that Big Al is fooling around with the "Muffler-Mate-Of-The-Month" and that he paid for her visit to an exclusive health spa, Judith follows her to the spa for the inevitable confrontation. Once there, however, she opens up to the lives of other women and in the course of events is boiled, steamed, exercized, massaged and lipo-sucked into self-realization. Samantha Eggars also stars.

"Round Numbers" co-stars Shani Wallis, Debra Christofferson, Kerry Remsen, Hope Marie Carlton and Natalie Barish.

Production credits include cinematography by Roger Olkowski, production design by Jonathan Carlson and set decoration by Nicki Roberts. The costumes were designed by Emelle Holmes and the editor is Rod Stephens, A.C.E.

# # #

What are some of the problems with this release? Let's check the first paragraph. Does it answer the five Ws?
√ **Who?** (We're not told)
√ **What?** Principal photography has been completed on "Round Numbers," a new feature film
√ **When?** (now [has been completed])
√ **Where?** Los Angeles (second paragraph)
√ **Why/how?** Written and directed by Nancy Zala and produced by Allan Mann

It is critical that all essential information is contained in the first paragraph. That's because the first paragraph is often the only paragraph that gets used by a newspaper. One way to check on your first paragraph is with the five Ws. Then you must ask yourself: will an editor find this release newsworthy? Finally you must ask yourself: if the first paragraph is all that gets used -- as is often the case -- will I have served the needs of my client, and will my client be satisfied?

This first paragraph fails the five Ws test. It also fails the news test. Remember, you're in competition with many other news releases. So ask yourself, What is compelling about this release? Not much. What would make it compelling? Names of stars, or, at least, recognizable actors. That would also answer the question: Who?

OK. Give me a name. Kate Mulgrew. That certainly answers the question: Who? But this can be tricky. There may be other names that should be included. Who about Samantha Eggar, Marty Ingels. Shani Wallis? All right.

What about the "What?" Even though we have some information, we don't have enough. Remember, we're trying to create interest in this film. What kind of film is it? A comedy! So, let's say that.

We should also say what the comedy is about. Now the third paragraph does that. But remember, the third paragraph may not get published. Then what? Also, the third paragraph is too long for a news release. It's more like a synopsis. You must come up with the essence of the story.   What's the comedy about? It's *about women in a health spa.*

We have all the elements now for our first paragraph except one: the name of the production company. Now let's try again.

<u>NEWS RELEASE</u>   <u>FOR IMMEDIATE RELEASE</u>

Contact: KATHY SHEPARD
             ROLF GOMPERTZ
             (818) 980-3576

'ROUND NUMBERS,' FEATURE FILM STARRING KATE MULGREW, SAMANTHA EGGAR, SHANI WALLIS, MARTY INGELS, COMPLETES PRINCIPAL PHOTOGRAPHY

Principal photography has been completed in Los Angeles on a comedy about women in a health spa, "Round Numbers," a new feature film from FilumThropix, inc., starring Kate Mulgrew, Samantha Eggar, Shani Wallis, and Marty Ingels, written and directed by Nancy Zala, and produced by Allan Mann.

Natalie Barish, Debra Christofferson, and Hope Marie Carlton also star in this rollicking, sophisticated comedy, which centers on a middle aged married woman who creates havoc in a posh health spa, when she revolts against what she considers to be the absurd, oppressive standards of physical beauty being foisted on women all their lives.

Roger Olkowski served as cinematographer. The feature was filmed in Hollywood by FilumThropix, inc., the independent production company headed by Zala, president, and Mann, vice president.

Jonathan Carlson served as production designer, Nicki Roberts as set decorator, Emelle Holmes, as costume designer, and Rod Stephens, A.C.E. as editor. Norman Mamey composed the music. Casting is by Barbara Remsen, C.S.A., Ann Remsen Manners, and Jeanne Ashby.

The film is scheduled to be shown distributors by mid-February.

# # #

1/14/91

NOTE: Please note special spelling of company name: FilumThropix, inc.

9

Δ **Test your release -- three basic questions.** Note the first paragraph. Ask yourself the three basic questions now: 1) Does it answer the 5 Ws? 2) Does it have news value? 3) Will your client be happy and have her needs met if nothing else appears in print? Yes, yes, yes.

Note the second paragraph and how the storyline has been condensed.

Note the final note at the bottom of the page. Whenever you have an unusual spelling, call attention to it, so that the editor won't "correct it."

Now note how Daily Variety and The Hollywood Reporter treated the story. How many paragraphs did they use? What information did they use? How much of that information was in the first paragraph?

Remember this example!

Wed., July 24, 1991   *VARIETY*

SHORT TAKES

*   *   *

Principal photography has been completed on ''Round Numbers,'' comedy about women in a health spa, new feature film from FilumThropix Inc. It stars Kate Mulgrew, Samantha Eggar, Shani Wallis and Marty Ingels. It's written and directed by Nancy Zala and produced by Allan Mann.

THE *Hollywood* REPORTER®   WEDNESDAY, JANUARY 23, 1991

FILM SHORTS

Production has wrapped in Los Angeles on FilumThropix's "Round Numbers," a health spa comedy featuring Kate Mulgrew, Samantha Eggar, Shani Wallis and Marty Ingels. FilumThropix president Nancy Zala wrote and directed the feature, which will be looking for a domestic distributor next month, and FilumThropix vp Allan Mann served as the producer.

I have one more example to share with you, a much more complex one. I was asked to handle the publicity when National Geographic Television opened a West Coast office in 1991. This called for a news release, to begin with. Following is the final release that I prepared and that was sent out.

NEWS
NATIONAL GEOGRAPHIC SOCIETY

<u>For Immediate Release</u>

NATIONAL GEOGRAPHIC TELEVISION, IN MAJOR NEW MOVE, OPENS OFFICE IN HOLLYWOOD

In a historic move, the National Geographic Society, which entered television in 1965, has opened its Hollywood office in Studio City, headed by multiple award-winning filmmaker Nicolas Noxon ("The Sharks," "Secrets of the *Titanic* "), Senior Producer, National Geographic Television.

He is joined by such Emmy winners as Producer Teresa Koenig, Supervising Editor Barry Nye, and Researcher/Script Editor Marjorie "Mickey" Moomey. The team also includes Associate Producer Kathryn Pasternak.

"The television division began with a staff of five," said Tom Simon, Executive in Charge of Production, National Geographic Television. "Today, we have over 100 individuals working in this area. We are excited about establishing a West Coast presence. While in the past we were limited to exclusive co-production deals, the opening of our office in Hollywood signals our openness to new ideas, to a variety of co-production arrangements with individuals and companies, and to direct involvement in all aspects of production."

"Post-production on most of our Specials, and some EXPLORER projects, will be done out of our Hollywood office. Also, we are glad to be near top filmmakers, composers and actors who often narrate our programs," added Noxon.

Today, National Geographic is the largest producer of documentaries in the U.S. National Geographic films are offered on commercial and non-commercial broadcast TV, cable television, home videocassette, and in international TV markets. National Geographic Television supplies 96 hours of premiere

TELEVISION DIVISION, NATIONAL GEOGRAPHIC SOCIETY, WASHINGTON, D. C.   20036   (202) 857-7000

programming annually, including the National Geographic Specials and National Geographic EXPLORER.

The Specials rank as one of the longest-running and most honored documentary film series ever produced, with four hour-long documentaries premiering annually on the Public Broadcasting Service and underwritten by Chevron.

The two-hour EXPLORER series brings the excitement and variety of *National Geographic* magazine to cable television. Seen each week on TBS, the two-hour program offers three to five films. In addition to National Geographic Society filmmakers, EXPLORER has created an important new outlet for talented film producers from around the world.

Since its start in 1965, National Geographic Television has received more than 450 broadcast awards, including 36 Emmys and three George Foster Peabody awards.

Nick Noxon is responsible for some of the most highly acclaimed films produced by National Geographic Television. He wrote and produced "The Sharks," a Special that aired in 1982 and still ranks as the highest-rated program ever to be broadcast by PBS. He also wrote and produced "Secrets of the *Titanic*," the ratings record-breaker* on National Geographic EXPLORER, which aired over cable's TBS in 1987 (*ranked by average-minute audience). Noxon wrote and produced three of the first Specials when they originally aired on CBS. Films produced, written and directed by Noxon have won virtually every award in American television and in film festivals around the world, including two Emmys and three George Foster Peabody Awards.

When Teri Koenig joined the National Geographic Specials in 1986, she was named associate producer of "Secrets of the *Titanic*," and received an Emmy for research she did for that show. She co-produced the National Geographic Special, "Splendid Stones." She brings a varied background in television and motion pictures to her current position. She served as associate producer with Churchill Entertainment on the NBC children's special, "The Silk King." She also worked four seasons as associate producer for Columbia Pictures Television on "Ripley's Believe It or Not," which aired on ABC. She has co-authored four books and authored three biographies.

Barry Nye was awarded an Emmy for the National Geographic Special, "Realm of the Alligator." He has served as supervising editor and film editor on 25 National Geographic Specials. He was also honored with three Eddies from the American Cinema Editors for his work on such Specials as "Cats: Caressing the Tiger," "Among the Wild Chimpanzees," and "The Explorers: A Century of Discovery." He also received the Wildscreen International Film Festival's Best Editing Award for "Land of the Tiger." Nye worked on the Specials at various PBS stations before joining National Geographic Television in February, 1991.

Mickey Moomey, who is also called "The TV Facts Lady" by her co-workers, came to work for the National Geographic Society in 1951. She has been a researcher/editor on 90 National Geographic TV documentaries and 12 "Decades of Decision" TV films for the U.S. Bicentennial. In 1990, she received an Emmy for her work on the "Elephant" Special.

Kathryn Pasternak joined National Geographic Television in 1991. Prior to that she was a writer/researcher for development of documentary television series for PBS and cable, with WQED/West. She also served as assistant producer with WQED/West on the National Geographic Television Special, "The Soul of Spain," and conducted all research and wrote the proposal for this project. Pasternak is a

Harvard graduate and the recipient of the Royal Society of Arts' Silver Medal, and an International Film Seminar grant.

The National Geographic Television office is located at 4370 Tujunga Ave., Ste. 300, Studio City (corner Moorpark), Calif. 91604. Phone number is: 818/506-8300.

# # #

July 1991

CONTACT
Rolf Gompertz,
Rolf Gompertz Communications
818/980-3576

Melissa Montefiore
Manager, Public Relations
Television Division
National Geographic Society
202/857-7627

It doesn't matter how big your client or how major your story is, the same principles, that we discussed previously, apply.

To begin with, give the story the basic 5 Ws test. Does it pass?

This is a long release, four pages, to be exact. Nobody expected any publication to run the full release. So why the length? For informational purposes essentially. For background, in case someone wants to know more or wants to develop a bigger story, now or later.

So how do you decide the order of things? By their importance and news value.

Please note also that the story contains two quotes. The first quote, in the third paragraph, also serves the purpose of attribution. We have a high-ranking executive elaborating on the announcement. This is followed by a quote from the person heading the West Coast office. Always make sure that you quote individuals in the order of rank, with the highest ranking corporate executive coming first. (Since this release, Nick Noxon and Tom Simon have each been named executive producer.)

Try to figure out now how much of this release, if anything, will get picked up by the media.

Δ **The writing process.** Before answering that question, let me return to the writing process. We are professional writers. That means we will rewrite and polish what we are working on until it meets our highest professional standards. Only then do we submit the material to our client for approval.

At this point we must be willing to rewrite further. A release may still go through several rewrites before it is finally approved for release to the media. That is part of the process. It is normal. It is nothing personal. It must be understood and accepted. Often there is more than one person involved who must sign off on a release. Each person may want to make one or more changes. Most of the time these changes are legitimate and perfectly appropriate. Remember, we are here to fulfill the needs and wishes of our client.

Sometimes we must advise a client against a particular change, for reasons of our own. If it is an important issue, it is worth standing our ground and arguing the point. If it's a minor issue, don't battle over it, just to get your way. Be flexible. That way, when you do have something to say, you will have greater credibility.

For instance, we discussed the wording: "has opened its Hollywood office in Studio City."

Why do you think this was questioned? What else could you have substituted for "Hollywood"? Why go with "Hollywood"? Why do you think the phrase stayed in the release instead of being changed to "has opened its office in Studio City"? Later on, when we look at the media stories, keep these questions in mind and see how they handled the information.

We are professional writers. Every word matters. Following is a paragraph by paragraph breakdown of the above news release and the final editing it went through. Note how subtle some of the changes are. When writing, pay attention to every word you use.

NATIONAL GEOGRAPHIC TELEVISION, IN MAJOR NEW MOVE, OPENS FIRST OFFICE IN HOLLYWOOD

In another historic move, the National Geographic, which entered television in 1965, has opened its first own Hollywood office in Studio City, headed by multiple award-winning filmmaker Nick Noxon ("The Sharks," "Secrets of the Titanic"), Senior Producer, National Geographic Television.

CHANGE:
6/21/91
>   delete: first own
>   Titanic to *Titanic*

7/9/91
>   ~~Nick~~ Nicolas

7/11/91
>   In a ~~nother~~ historic move

7/12/91
>   In an historic move, the National Geographic <u>Society</u>

He is joined by such Emmy winners as producer/Associate Producer Teri Koenig, Supervising Editor Barry Nye, and Researcher/Script Editor Marjorie "Mickey" Moomey. The team includes Associate Producer Kathryn Pasternak, a Harvard graduate and the recipient of the Royal Society of Arts Silver Medal and International Film Seminar grant.

CHANGE:
6/21/91
>   delete: Harvard graduate....International Film seminar grant (add to biographical paragraph later in release)

7/9/91
>   ~~Teri~~ Teresa

7/11/91
>   The team <u>also</u> includes

7/12/91
>   He is joined by such Emmy winners as Producer~~/Associate Producer~~

"We launched our move into television on the West Coast in 1965," said Tim Kelly, vice president and director of National Geographic Television. "The television division began with a staff of ??. Today, we are the largest producer of documentaries in the U.S., and the second largest in the world. Since we began, we have received more than 450 broadcast awards, including 36 Emmys and three George Foster Peabody awards. While in the past we were limited to exclusive co-production deals, the opening of our own office in Hollywood signals our openness to new ideas, to co-production arrangements with qualified individuals and companies, and to direct involvement in all aspects of production."

CHANGE:
6/21/91
    ...to a variety of co-production arrangements with ~~qualified~~ individuals and companies...

7/9/91
    ~~Since we began, we have received more than 450 broadcast awards, including 36 Emmys and three George Foster Peabody awards.~~
    ...the opening of our ~~own~~ office

7/11/91

    ~~We launched our move into television on the West Coast in 1965~~
Change attribution from Tim Kelly to Tom Simon, Executive in Charge of Production.

7/12/91
    "The television division began with a staff of <u>five</u>...

Added Noxon: "All post-production on our specials, and some other projects, now will be done out of our Hollywood office. Also, we would be glad to hear from agents of stars who would be interested in narrating our programs.

CHANGE:
6/21/91
    "~~All~~ Post-production <u>on most of</u> our specials, and some 'EXPLORER' projects...

7/9/91
    ...and some EXPLORER projects ~~now~~ will be done

7/11/91
    ~~Added Noxon:~~
    ~~Also, we would be glad to hear from agents of stars who would be interested in narrating our programs.~~

19

Change to: Also, we are glad to be near top filmmakers, composers and actors who often narrate our programs," added Noxon.

ADD:

National Geographic films are now offered on commercial and non-commercial broadcast TV, cable television, home videocassette, and in international TV markets. Today, national Geographic is the largest producer of documentaries in the U.S., supplying 96 hours of premiere programming annually, including ~~the~~ National Geographic Specials and National Geographic ~~Explorer~~ EXPLORER.

7/11/91

. National Geographic films are ~~now~~ offered
Rearrange paragraph:

Today, National Geographic is the largest producer of documentaries in the U.S. National Geographic films are offered on commercial and non-commercial broadcast TV, cable television, home videocassette, and in international TV markets. National Graphic Television supplies 96 hours of premiere programming annually, including the National Geographic Specials and National Geographic EXPLORER.

The Specials rank as one of the longest-running and most honored documentary film series ever produced, with four hour-long documentaries premiering annually on the Public Broadcasting Service and underwritten by Chevron.

The two-hour EXPLORER series brings the excitement and variety of National Geographic magazine to cable television. Seen each week on TBS, the two-hour program offers three to five films. In addition to national Geographic Society filmmakers, EXPLORER has created an important new outlet for talented film producers from around the world.

7/11/91

National Geographic magazine

Since its start in 1965, National Geographic Television has received more than 450 broadcast awards, including 36 Emmys and three George Foster Peabody awards.

Noxon is responsible for some of the most highly acclaimed films produced by National Geographic Television. He wrote and produced "The Sharks," a Special that aired in 1982 and still ranks as the highest-rated program ever to be broadcast by PBS. He also wrote and produced "Secrets of the Titanic ," the ratings record-breaker* on National EXPLORER, which

20

aired over cable's TBS in 1987 (*ranked by average-minute audience). Noxon wrote and produced three of the first Specials when they originally aired on CBS. Films produced, written and directed by Noxon have won virtually every award in American television and in film festivals around the world, including two Emmys and three George Foster Peabody Awards.

CHANGE:

6/21/91

    <u>Nick</u> Noxon

    "Secrets of the *Titanic* "

7/12/91

    on National <u>Geographic</u> EXPLORER

    When Teri Koenig joined the National Geographic Specials in 1986, she was named associate producer of "Secrets of the *Titanic* ," and received an Emmy for research she did for that show. She brings a varied background in television and motion pictures to her current position. She served as associate producer with Churchill Entertainment on the NBC children's special, "The Silk King." She also worked four seasons as associate producer for Columbia Pictures Television on "Ripley's Believe It or Not," which aired on ABC. She has co-authored four books and authored three biographies.

CHANGE:

7/12/91

Add: <u>...and received an Emmy for research she did for that show. She co-produced the National Geographic Special, "Splendid Stones."</u>

    Barry Nye was awarded an Emmy for the National Geographic Special, "Realm of the Alligator." He has served as supervising editor and film editor on 25 National Geographic Specials. He was also honored with three Eddies from the American Cinema Editors for his work on such NG Specials as "Cats: Caressing the Tiger," "Chimpanzees," and "The Explorers: A Century of Discovery." He also received the Wildscreen International Film Festival's Best Editing Award for "Land of the Tiger." Nye worked on the NG Specials at various PBS stations before joining National Geographic Television in February, 1991.

CHANGE:

6/21/91

"Among the Wild Chimpanzees"

7/9/91

~~NG~~ Specials as "Cats:..."   ~~NG~~ Specials at various...

"Mickey" Moomey, who is also called "Queen of Facts" by her co-workers, came to work for the National Geographic Society in 1951. She has been a researcher/editor on 90 National Geographic TV documentaries and 12 "Decades of Decision" TV films for the U.S. Bicentennial. In 1990, she received an Emmy for her work on the "Elephant" special.

CHANGE:

6/21/91

Mickey

~~"Queen of Facts"~~ "The TV Facts Lady"

on the "Elephant" Special

Kathryn Pasternak joined National Geographic Television in 1991. Prior to that she was a writer/researcher for development of documentary television series for PBS and cable, with WQED/West.   She also served as assistant producer with WQED/West on the National Geographic Television Special, "The Soul of Spain," and conducted all research and wrote the proposal for this project.

CHANGE:

6/21/91

Pasternak is a Harvard graduate and the recipient of the Royal Society of Arts' Silver Medal, and an International Film Seminar grant.

The National Geographic Television office is located at 4370 Tujunga Ave., Ste. 300, Studio City (corner Moorpark). Phone number is: 818/506-8300.

CHANGE:

7/9/91

(corner Moorpark), Calif. 91604.

Δ **Now for the results.** We are looking at four different trade publications. How much of the first paragraph was used? The second? The third? The fourth? The fifth? Was anything used beyond the fifth paragraph? Did the very last paragraph get used? Is it ever used? Why include it? Why not mention all the information of the last paragraph in the first paragraph instead? Were any of the quotes used? Why? How did each published report describe the office location? Do you think the client was satisfied with each of these media breaks? Why?

SHORT TAKES

The National Geographic Society has opened a West Coast office in Studio City, headed by Nicolas Noxon, senior producer for National Geo-graphic TV. National Geographic currently produces the "Explorer" series as well as its noted docu specials and said it's also open to co-productions. Producer Teresa Koenig, supervising editor Barry Nye, researcher Marjorie (Mickey) Moomey and associate producer Kathryn Pasternak join Noxon in the new office.

* * *

THE REPORTER ®

THURSDAY, JULY 18, 1991

TV TALK

The National Geographic Society, which entered TV in 1965, has opened a Hollywood office in Studio City, headed by filmmaker Nicolas Noxon ("The Sharks," "Secrets of the Titanic").

The new office will look for co-production deals with individuals and companies for future National Geographic productions.

As an added benefit of the step, postproduction on most National Geographic specials will be handled out of the Hollywood facility.

* * *

THE PRODUCTION MAGAZINE

VOLUME 8   ISSUE 8

TELEPRODUCTIONS

The largest producer of documentaries in the U.S., National Geographic Television (NGT) opened a West Coast production office in Studio City, Calif. Headed by award-winning filmmaker and NGT senior producer Nicolas Noxon, the new location opens NGT to new co-production agreements and will serve as the post-production site for most of National Geographic's one-hour specials and some of its "Explorer" projects. Also based in the new office are producer Teresa Koenig, associate producer Kathryn Pasternak, supervising editor Barry Nye and researcher/script editor Marjorie "Mickey" Moomey.

The Industry

National Geo Goes West

■ National Geographic Television, producer of the famed National Geographic specials and the *Explorer* series, has opened a West Coast headquarters. The Studio City, California, office, which will supervise post-production on most specials and some *Explorer* projects, is headed by senior producer Nicolas Noxon.

"We're excited about establishing a West Coast presence," says Tom Simon, executive in charge of production for National Geographic TV. "While in the past we were limited to exclusive coproduction deals, the opening of our Hollywood office signals our openness to a variety of coproduction arrangements with individuals and companies and to direct involvement in all aspects of production."

The National Geographic Society entered television in 1965. Today the TV unit supplies some 100 hours of original programming annually.

— *Eds.*

Δ **Types of news releases.** The announcement story and the follow-up story represent two types of news releases. The subject matter could involve an event, corporate news or programming news.

For instance, a network may decide to put a new series, a TV movie, or a special on the air. This calls for an announcement story. Often, all the information is not available at this point. Stars, guest stars, or additional cast members may still have to be determined. The broadcast date may not be set yet. When these things happen, you issue one or more follow-up stories. Finally, when you launch your full publicity campaign, you must also send out a format story, usually about a month before airdate. The format story is different from an announcement story or follow-up story, and will be discussed in a separate chapter. When time is short, an announcement story and format story may be combined.

Let's look at the announcement story for "Wake, Rattle & Roll."

'WAKE, RATTLE & ROLL' SET TO PREMIERE SEPTEMBER 17
<u>WITH A FAST-PACED MIX OF LIVE-ACTION, ANIMATRONICS AND ANIMATION</u>
<u>Produced by Hanna-Barbera and Worldvision Enterprises,
Daily Syndicated Children's Series is Uniquely
Designed for Morning Slots</u>

"Wake, Rattle & Roll," a new daily half-hour series
combining live-action, animatronics and world-premiere animation,
is set to debut September 17. Already cleared in over 75% of the
country, including 29 of the top 30 markets, the program
represents a revolutionary concept in television as the only
nationally syndicated children's show targeted exclusively for
air in the morning time periods and tailored to the unique
lifestyle of kids.

The series kicks off its first season with a prime access
half-hour sneak preview special which airs in the window of
August 26 - September 16. "Wake, Rattle & Roll" is produced by
Hanna-Barbera and Worldvision Enterprises, Inc. in association
with Four Point Entertainment.

"Wake, Rattle & Roll," which was created by Hanna-Barbera
president and chief executive officer David Kirschner ("An
American Tail," "Child's Play"), continues the company's
tradition of developing programming which both entertains and
educates. "Our goal is to provide a fun, imaginative and

(more...)

Hanna-Barbera Productions. Inc. 3400 Cahuenga Blvd., Los Angeles. CA 90068 • Phone: (213)851-5000 • Fax (213)969-
Worldvision Enterprises, Inc. 660 Madison Ave.. New York. NY 10021 • Phone: (212)832-3838 • Fax (212)980-5970

educational show that will become a morning routine for kids around the country. It should be the last thing they do before leaving for school or camp," says Executive Producer Kirschner.

"Stations and viewers alike are seeking quality children's programming," comments John D. Ryan, president and chief executive officer of Worldvision Enterprises, Inc. "No national show since the popular 'Captain Kangaroo' has established a franchise in early morning, and with the current competition for afternoon slots such that it is, we felt the timing was right to launch 'Wake, Rattle & Roll' with an eye on morning periods."

The host of "Wake, Rattle & Roll" is Sam, an off-the-wall 14-year-old played by popular teen actor R.J. Williams, who is joined by viewers in his basement bedroom every morning as he's getting ready for school. Sam's animatronic sidekick is a fast-talking, videocassette-headed robot named DECKS (Digital Electrosonic Cassette-Headed Kinetic System), part computer, VCR and television, invented by Sam's eccentric scientist grandfather, Dr. Lester T. Quirk (played by veteran comic actor Avery Schreiber). Sam and DECKS engage in a variety of high energy and often unexpected activities, using odds and ends found in their basement paradise to get themselves out of sticky situations or simply have fun.

Some of the gizmos the pair creates and uses on a regular basis include The People Processor, a gadget which can bring people or objects back from the past; the Living Library, which allows Sam to enter a book, or brings literary characters into his basement; and the Mondo View, a giant screen which can

(more...)

broadcast Grandpa Quirk from any part of the world. Sam and DECKS also participate in some pretty crazy Remote Fights when the two grab their remote controls and zap each other into other recognizable real and animated characters.

"Wake, Rattle & Roll" will also feature two all-new cartoons. "Monster Tails" chronicles the antics of pets who have been left behind in a creepy castle when their masters leave for Hollywood. "Fender Bender 500" reintroduces some classic Hanna-Barbera characters in a contemporary setting as they race through a different country each day, and highlights information about geography. Among the 4X4 vehicle drivers are Yogi Bear, Huckleberry Hound, Quick Draw McGraw and Snagglepuss.

Currently featured in a recurring role in the ABC-TV daytime drama "General Hospital," R.J. Williams has guest starred in numerous prime time television series including "21 Jump Street," "Star Trek: The Next Generation," "Magnum P.I.," "Highway to Heaven" and "St. Elsewhere." He has also acted alongside Anthony Quinn in the motion picture "Men of Passion," Robert Wagner in the miniseries "Windmills of the Gods," and Jaclyn Smith in the telefilm "The Night They Saved Christmas." He also does the voice-overs for the new animated Disney series, "Tale Spin."

Ron Ziskin and Shukri Ghalayini of Four Point Entertainment are co-executive producers. Sam Ewing and Glenn Leopold of Hanna-Barbera are executives in charge of production for "Wake, Rattle & Roll," and Kelly Ward is head writer.

(more...)

"Wake, Rattle & Roll" is produced by Hanna-Barbera and Worldvision Enterprises, Inc., in association with Four Point Entertainment. Hanna-Barbera is a totally owned subsidiary of the Great American Broadcasting Company (GABC). Worldvision Enterprises, Inc., the world's leading distributor for independent television producers, is a unit of Spelling Entertainment, Inc.

# # #

CONTACTS: Peter Berk   Mitch Zamarin
          Jan Fisher   Marisa Spitz
          THE LIPPIN GROUP/LA   THE LIPPIN GROUP/NY
          (213) 965-1990   (212) 986-7080

          Sarah Baisley
          HANNA-BARBERA
          (213) 969-1211

071790jcf

Δ **Note the use of a double headline, when necessary.** Chances are no editor will use such a double headline. Its purpose is to provide the editor with all the important information at a glance.

Δ **Note how carefully the first paragraph has been crafted.** There are lots of buzz words here: *new...daily...half-hour series...combining live-action, animatronics and world-premiere animation...cleared in over 75% of the country, including 29 of the top 30 markets...revolutionary concept..the only nationally syndicated children's show targeted exclusively for air in the morning time periods...tailored to the unique lifestyle of kids.*

Δ **This is actually a double announcement story.** It announces the series, set to debut September 17, as mentioned in the first paragraph, and it announces a prime access half-hour sneak preview special (note the wording) to air between August 26 and September 16, as mentioned in the second paragraph. The second paragraph, therefore, is still part of the first paragraph, because of this. Don't ever forget to work your client's name into your first paragraph. Note how this has been done here.

The tendency is to start the first paragraph with your client's name. In this case, the client, Hanna-Barbera, has wisely resisted that tendency. You should start with what is most newsworthy. *The new daily half-hour series, "Wake, Rattle & Roll,"* is what's most newsworthy and that's what this news release starts with.

Notice how well the rest of the release is crafted. It doesn't depend on hype, but on impressive facts and information. See how you give a news release prestige through association ("An American Tail," "Child's Play," "Captain Kangaroo").

Study the quotes. See how carefully they have been worked out. These are good, functional quotes. What is their function? Why is Kirschner quoted before Ryan? When might you reverse this order?

We now learn that popular teen actor R.J. Williams and veteran comic actor Avery Schreiber appear in the series. Why are they mentioned here? Could they have been mentioned earlier? Why might you have done so? How?

You are constantly making choices, consciously and subconsciously. There should be a good, professional reason for all your choices of words, information and placement. There are few absolutes.

What about the two all-new cartoons, mentioned on page 3? Why here? Make a good case.

Note the paragraph about R. J. Williams. Why these credits only? Why TV before film? Why the reference to Disney?

The next to the last paragraph contains the major staff production credits. They should be part of the release, but not the main part -- unless you are writing a release aimed primarily at the trade publications rather than the consumer publications. The final paragraph contains the standard corporate information, used primarily as a matter of record. It, too, is generally of interest only to trade publications.

The contact information at the end lets you know that there is an agency involved in this project and the media may make contact with Hanna-Barbera on the West Coast or the agency on either coast.

The code at the bottom of the page indicates the date the release was sent out and the person who wrote it.

What else do you notice about the way the pages and the headlines have been set up? How are show titles written? Study everything. Spelling, punctuation, abbreviations, capitalization. You will soon notice that organizations differ markedly in style.

3

BIOGRAPHIES

Δ **Types.** Biographies come in various shapes and sizes, depending on their purpose. There are one-paragraph biographies, half-page biographies, one-, two-, three- and-more-page biographies.

There are biographies that are essentially just a stringing together of credits and there are other biographies that give you a real sense of who the person is.

There are biographies that are structured for television publicity and there are biographies that are structured for motion picture publicity.

Δ **Purpose.** Biographies seldom, if ever, get published. They serve a different purpose. In whatever form, biographies provide the media with background information. They point out career highlights, personal details, and insights into the individual. They provide an interviewer with "angles," that is, areas of interest to be explored.

MINI-BIO Let's begin with the shortest biography, the thumbnail sketch, or **"The Sun** mini-bio. Note the ones written for "The Sun Also Rises," a **Also Rises"** four-hour miniseries which aired on NBC Monday Night at the Movies. These bios consist of two segments: the first contains the name of the star, the name of the character portrayed, and a brief description of this character. The second segment consists of major film credits, followed by television credits.

Since this is a TV movie (or miniseries) the more prestigious film credits precede the television credits. Note how specially identifying credits, whether film or television, are highlighted (Leonard Nimoy as Spock, Hart Bochner as the son of Lloyd Bochner, and Ian Charleson as the runner in "Chariots of Fire.") The point of all this is to bring essential information quickly into focus for the benefit of reviewers, writers, and print or broadcast interviewers. These mini-bios are nine to 12 lines in length.

Notice the style -- what is capitalized, what is underlined, and how credits are written and punctuated. The lines are single-spaced. This is NBC style.
A good way to determine what goes into these mini-bios is to ask the individuals involved, or their agents, what they consider to be their most important credits. This is especially helpful when there are a lot of credits to choose from. Also, some of the credits may look better than they are (the role was cut in the editing, the actor prefers another show over this one, the film was a critical success but not a commercial success, or vice versa).

A press kit also often calls for mini-bios of the major staff people involved: executive producer, producer, director, writer and possibly others. These bios, like the celebrity mini-bios, single out those elements which are most recognizable and arresting. These bios are different in the way they are set up from the celebrity bios -- the name and title of the individual is over the thumbnail sketch, with the name capitalized but not underlined. This is NBC style.

"Sarah, Plain And Tall" Compare the previous mini-bios with those written for "Sarah, Plain and Tall," a Hallmark Hall of Fame presentation on CBS. These bios contain a bit more biographical information. They are up to two lines longer, for the major stars. The other performers get around eight lines. However, there is no character description. Also, the name of the character is placed in parentheses.

The style is the same for performer- and staff-bios: names are capitalized and underlined, and the character or title follow in parentheses. HALLMARK HALL OF FAME is capitalized but not placed in parentheses. Book titles are underlined. The copy is single-spaced.

ONE-PAGE BIO "Cheers" The one-page bio runs 25 lines, give or take a line. It is used by the network in the annual press kits. It is well suited for dramatic and comedy series, and their frequently large casts. NBC's "Cheers" is a good example.

The name of the star, character, series, time and network are contained in the head. The body of the bio consists of tell-tale personal elements and credits. The first paragraph offers the most intriguing, eye-catching, and latest information. The rest of the bio follows a chronological format and is written in narrative form. A quote helps personalize and humanize the bio. Look for some quotes and see how they are used.

When a series goes longer than one season, these bios should be updated every year. Note how this has been done here.

Biographical summaries at the end of the bio were customary once. Many PR departments have eliminated them. The summaries are to biographies what fact sheets are to news releases -- they provide a quick overview and basic statistics at a glance.

It is typical of show business bios that they will mention the date and month of birth, but not the year. The reason is obvious: we are living in a youth-oriented society where growing older is perceived as a negative. Actors, like everyone else, worry about job opportunities. It shouldn't be that way, but it is. That's the reality. The media have other ways of finding out an actor's age, and they usually do, if they want that information. Sometimes the actors will mention their age to an interviewer, if asked. But, as a general rule, PR people withhold that information from the bios, for the reasons stated.

Δ **As for other bios, they can be divided into two categories: short bios and long (or, full) bios.** Each has advantages and disadvantages.

√   Short bios can be read and absorbed much more quickly than long bios. They also cut down on expenses (they don't cost as much to print and mail).

√   Long bios, on the other hand, provide the media with a much more comprehensive picture of your stars, their lives, and their work. They allow for more quotes and anecdotes.

SHORT BIO Let's first take a look at some short biographies, including the
Eva LaRue following one on Eva LaRue, which I wrote for The Brokaw
Company and King World, when I was retained to do the press kit for the new, syndicated "Candid Camera" series, with host Dom DeLuise.

EVA
Biography

They call her Eva. That's fine with her.

In fact, actress Eva La Rue is all smiles these days. And why not? After all, she's on "CANDID CAMERA."

"I cried when I got the job," said the vivacious performer, who is billed simply as Eva, host Dom Deluise's sidekick, on the new syndicated, half-hour series.

Fans of the NBC-TV daytime series, "SANTA BARBARA," will remember her in the role of Margo Collins, the good girl with a bad past, whom she portrayed during most of 1988.

Eva, who is in her early twenties, has been performing since she was four years old, when her mom, Marcie La Rue, enrolled her in a dance class.

"It wasn't so much the acting bug as the entertaining bug that bit me," said Eva. "From the time I started dancing, I knew I wanted to be an entertainer."

At the age of six, she was named Little Miss California. At 14, she was one of six California talent show winners flown to Washington, D.C. to perform at the White House, where she sang for First Lady Nancy Reagan. At 16, Eva won the title of Miss American Teenager.

"I love to compete," said Eva, who was on her way to the Miss USA competition after winning the Miss Riverside County title, when she got her first motion picture break, a co-starring role in "THE BARBARIANS."

A more recent motion picture, "HEART CONDITION," offered her a more challenging role, that of a heroin addict. She played a robot in the film "CRASH & BURN," for cable and home video, and will appear as an anchor woman in "Robocop III."

more...

She has guest starred on many television shows and co-hosted a cable show for Disney, "VIDEOPOLIS," a variety program for youngsters under 15 years of age. She also co-hosted an entertainment news program on the cable channel Movietime.

Eva was born December 27 in Long Beach, Calif., and raised on a one-acre ranch in Norco (Riverside county), Calif., a rural area, with bridal trails for streets, and hitching posts and water troughs at the local stores.

"If I could not be an entertainer, I'd want to be a horse trainer," said Eva, who grew up around horses, training and showing them in competition. "I had my first pony when I was four years old. Horses gave me my first sense of working from the ground up, making something out of nothing and not giving up."

Though allergic to horses, she won't stay away from them. Her current love is a horse called Exclusive Music, which she bought for $1500 and which is now worth $30,000. "Music" lives in Norco with its trainer, but Eva still rides and shows the horse.

Eva's family includes a sister, Nika, who is a fashion model, a half-brother, Luis Jr., 4, a half-sister, Lara, 8, and a late brother Chuck, 21, who died in a car accident.

"There were some lean times growing up in a single parent home," said Eva. "When I couldn't drive yet, Mom would drive me back and forth to Los Angeles, 70 miles each way, so I could go on interviews. I credit my mom for making my career possible. I'm really grateful to her."

# # #

Contact: Sanford Brokaw, The Brokaw Company, (213) 273-2060
          Allyson Kossow, King World (212) 315-4000

Δ **Elements.** There are certain elements I strive for, whether writing a short or long bio. They are:

- A punchy opening sentence, or paragraph, that captures the essence of the person or the situation. It should intrigue, provoke, or amuse.
- A fascinating, perhaps startling quote, as quickly as possible, for a direct connection between your subject and the reader.
- Reference to something topical, to show that there is something timely and newsworthy involved (this is usually a show that you are publicizing)
- An outstanding credit or two, up front, that gives the person credibility and makes the individual immediately recognizable.
- Short words, short sentences and short paragraphs. Short words, sentences and paragraphs give writing power. They are also easier to read and comprehend.
- Quotes alternating with narrative. This provides a change of rhythm and makes reading more interesting.
- Lots of good quotes. Quotes humanize your biography. They allow the person to speak directly to the reader. They allow you, the writer, to give the biography feeling and emotion, which, as a journalist/PR writer, you may not inject into the piece directly.
- First set up the story with all the essential details mentioned above; then proceed chronologically with it (it makes for easier understanding of the person's life and career).
- Avoid giving your own opinion. Don't editorialize. Paint the picture with selective facts and feelings (quotes). Don't tell, illustrate.
- Find something specific that will give your bio a perfect ending; avoid corny generalizations that could apply to anyone.
- Watch your sentence structure.
- Respect the meaning of words.
- Write tight. Find the precise word. Use one word instead of two or more.
- When in doubt, check it out (facts, spellings).
- Proof-read everything -- twice!

Δ **Sources of information.** When I do a biography, I ask for as much background information about the individual as possible: an existing bio, credits, clippings, reviews, and any publicity material. These come from the actor or actress, press agent, manager, agent, studio, network, production company, or agency. Sometimes the material is plentiful and helpful, at other times there is little, if any, material available.

Δ **Determining the approach.** After I have studied the material, I think about the person and the approach I want to take. I make a list of questions. Some are basic questions of fact, which are necessary but not stimulating. Some are questions designed to elicit an interesting response. Remember, however, that you're a press agent, not a reporter, and when you are told things that might prove embarrassing or hurtful, don't use it, even if the person has said it. If in doubt, ask if you may use it. In some cases, you must actually protect individuals against themselves.

Δ **List of questions.** In Eva's case, I only had bare credits to work from. I also found out that she'd been in some beauty contests. So, thinking about some of the show's she'd been on and "Candid Camera," her new show, I prepared the following list of questions:

1. What do you do on this show?
2. How did this job come about for you?
3. How do you spell your name (very important, even when it's an ordinary name, like, Sandi. Maybe it's spelled Sandee. Smith could be Smyth.)
4. Place of birth; date
5. Name of parents. Living? Dead? Married, divorced?
6. Any brothers or sisters? (You may wish to explore this and use it, or just make brief reference to it in the bio)
7. Where were you born and raised?
8. Where did you go to school.
9. Where do you live now, and with whom?
10. Tell me about some of the roles you did (you may ask about specific shows, such as "Santa Barbara," in this case). What happened to the character? Did any of those roles come about in an unusual way?
11. If the person was in a series, ask how long, and if they are still connected with that series.
12. How would you describe yourself? (Surprise questions -- the kind that people don't ask or that come at unexpected times in an interview -- will get a spontaneous, refreshing response).
13. Did you ever watch the old "Candid Camera"? If so, elaborate.
14. Did you ever work with Dom DeLuise? Anything funny happen when you met him now, or when you worked with him so far?
15. Has she traveled with the show? Where? Any anecdotes?
16. What was your first acting role? Or, what was the first time you gave a performance? How did that happen? Did anything unusual happen?
17. Tell me about winning the title of Miss American Teenager.
18. Did you ever consider going on to the Miss America contest?
19. What's the silliest role you ever had?
20. What's been your most satisfying role, and why?
21. What was your hardest role?
22. What would you like to do professionally?
23. If you couldn't act, what would be your second choice?
24. Are you a collector? What do you collect?

25. Do you have any favorite objects around the house?
26. Do you have a favorite saying? (Advice that was given to you or some words of wisdom that have come in handy?)
27. Is there some special thought that helps you when things are tough? What pulls you through?
28. What about marriage, children?
29. Is there anything you're afraid of?
30. What do you do for fun?
31. What's the hardest thing about acting?
32. What gives, and has given you, the greatest satisfaction?
33. Any hobbies? Favorite book, food? Favorite song? Favorite color? Why?
33. What haven't we covered that you'd like me to know about?

If you come armed with 25 to 30 questions, you'll get enough material for a good biography. The person may not have an answer -- or a good answer -- for every question, but that's OK. Interviewing is exploring. Be prepared to go down some unanticipated paths, especially if you think it's going to be interesting. You'll know what questions to ask when that happens. This is part of the fun and satisfaction of interviewing.

Paramount Studios Television handles its short bios differently from NBC. For one thing, they are double spaced. Also, the network carrying the series and the studio producing it are mentioned in the first paragraph. Compare this approach to that of NBC and the "Cheers" bios. By avoiding show information in the body of the story, the "Cheers" bio allows more room for biographical information. The Paramount bio, on the other hand, makes it easier for a writer to remember to credit the studio and network. A short biography runs anywhere from two to three pages.

Timothy Daly "Wings"   Take a look at the first paragraph of the Timothy Daly bio. See what the writer has done to create interest in Daly. What human interest factor has she introduced in the second paragraph? Is this something a writer or talk show host might want to explore? What other human interest factors do you find in the rest of the bio? If you wanted to add quotes to this biography and expand the human interest elements, what questions might you ask?

Of interest is the contact information at the end of the bio. The first reference is to the agency publicist who prepared the bio and press kit material and who probably also handles the publicity for the series. The second reference is to the publicity department head of the studio producing the series. This lets the media know whom to contact for additional information or interviews.

LONG (FULL) BIOGRAPHIES   Long, or full, biographies will run four to six pages, or even longer. I remember reading one that was 15 pages long, single-spaced! Once you go that far, you might as well keep going and write a book. Whether anyone, besides your client and his mother, would be thrilled, is another question.

Michele   The following Michele Lee bio from Bob Palmer Public Relations
Lee   is a typical "long" bio. Notice two things. It is an updated bio,
               written for the thirteenth season of the series, 'Knots Landing,"
               in which Michele Lee stars.

Here is a good example of the difference between network and agency bios. The network, as we have seen with other bios, will probably do a one- or two-page bio of its series' stars, while the agency will do a longer bio. Since TV editors will usually receive bios from both sources, they have the benefit of a short and long bio.

This bio serves one other purpose, namely, to call attention to an upcoming TV-movie, "My Son Johnny," and another upcoming project, Neil Simon's "Broadway Bound."

It's important to revise such bios after dated events (such as the TV-movie) so that an editor has accurate information. At all times, date your bio at the end, as has been done here (9/9l), so that an editor will always know how current a bio is and can then make the necessary editorial adjustments.

When there is nothing specific to which to call attention, you can write a more generic bio. Such a bio should always establish the essence of the person and their achievements, before proceeding in chronological order with their life and work.

BOB PALMER PUBLIC RELATIONS, INC.
1034 LAS PULGAS ROAD
PACIFIC PALISADES, CA 90272
TEL: 213-454-5118 FAX: 213-454-5249

MICHELE LEE
Biography

Michele Lee stars as Karen MacKenzie in "Knots Landing," now in its thirteenth season on the CBS Television Network. For her work she has been nominated for an Emmy as Best Actress [lead role, drama series], was named Actress of the Year by Gannett Newspapers, and Best Prime Time Actress in the 1992 Soap Opera Digest Awards.

Last year she was critically acclaimed for her portrayal of a blue collar woman tormented by tragedy of her own making in the CBS Movie "My Son Johnny." This year year she will be seen as Blanche in Neil Simon's "Broadway Bound," starring Anne Bancroft and Hume Cronin.

Michele has been directing for several years and helms several episodes of "Knots Landing" each season. In 1989 she produced and starred in the CBS Television movie "Single Women, Married Men." In 1990 she starred in "The Fatal Image," a thriller produced in Paris for CBS-TV.

With a body of work that includes a long-running series, hit Broadway musicals, feature films, TV movies, specials, recordings, producing and directing, Michele still exudes all of the cheerful enthusiasm that put her into professional ranks when she was a teenager. Privately, she is active in movements which address human needs and the quality of life on Earth.

41

She recently became a member of the Artists Committee of the John F. Kennedy Center for the Performing Arts, assisting the Board of Trustees in selecting Honorees.

Michele was born in Los Angeles on June 24, the first of two children of Sylvia and Jack Dusick, both now deceased. Her brother Kenneth B. Dusick is an attorney. Her dad was a make-up artist based primarily at the studio where "Knots Landing" has been filmed since 1979.

She was a performer from the start. At 3 she was singing for the family. At Louis Pasteur Junior High and Hamilton High she sang at school assemblies. By 16 she was a semi-professional band singer. Days after graduating, she went to her first open audition for a spot in a musical revue. She sang "You Make Me Feel So Young" with a tag ending. They said they'd call her, and call her they did.

The revue was "Vintage 60" and Michele's number was "Five Piece Band and a Woman Who Sings the Blues," a show stopper. Eight months later producer David Merrick brought the revue to New York where it closed after a short run.

Michele was back in L.A. doing another revue when she learned that they were looking for an an Italian-American type girl in New York to play the ingenue lead in a new musical, "Bravo Giovanni," to star Cesare Siepe of the Metropolitan Opera. She flew back, tried out, and won the role of a girl visiting Italy, the home of her parents, and falling for an older man. She was 18.

She went from "Bravo" to the smash hit musical "How to
Succeed in Business Without Really Trying," opposite Robert .
Morse, playing the full two-year run and and later starring with
Morse in the 1967 movie version. Television variety shows were
big at the time, and Michele was in demand, working with such
legends as Fred Astaire, Bob Hope and Dick Van Dyke. She did an
album for Columbia, "A Taste for the Fantastic," which broke for
a hit, as did her single, "L. David Sloane." Between movie and
TV appearances, she mounted a night club act which played Las
Vegas and New York. In 1969, she had two major features in
release, "The Love Bug" opposite Dean Jones, and Carl Reiner's
cult classic "The Comic" in which she revealed strength as a
dramatic actress opposite Dick Van Dyke and Mickey Rooney. It
was also the year Michele and James Farentino, whom she married
in 1966, became the parents of David Farentino, now 22. (Michele
and Jim divorced in 1981].

In 1973 Michele was back on Broadway with Tommy Tune and
Ken Howard in the musical "Seesaw," another hit. Said Clive
Barnes in the N.Y. Times, "Miss Lee proved a delicious mixture of
both the tough and vulnerable, with a show-biz passion that was
absolutely exultant." Said John Simon in New York Magazine, "She
sings, moves, acts and radiates like a true pentathlon champion,
deserving five-fold accolades." T.E. Kalem in TIME wrote, "Apart
from notable strength, the sheer likability of Michele Lee is
infectious." Mort Young of Hearst Newspapers wrote, "After the
opening performance, someone should have pinned a silver star on

Michele Lee's dressing room door, planted a kiss on her cheek and handed her the keys to the city."

For "Seesaw" she received the Drama Desk Award, the Outer Circle Critics Award and a Tony nomination.

Her next dramatic role was in the three-hour NBC Television presentation of "Dark Victory" with Anthony Hopkins and Elizabeth Montgomery, followed by "Bud and Lou," in which she played Anne, wife of comic Lou Costello. In 1985 she starred in NBC's "A Letter to Three Wives" with Loni Anderson and Stephanie Zimbalist.

Michele cherishes her career, but family comes first. Friendships run deep and are lasting. Her best friend in high school is her closest friend today. She has forty photo albums filled with five generations of family and friends. Her home is the setting for the holiday celebrations. Relationships change, but rarely end; she and Jim Farentino have remaioned friends.

On September 27, 1987, Michele married Fred Rappoport, a network executive and producer. The couple met in New York when Fred filled in for a friend with whom Michele had a date to go to the theatre. They have been together ever since.

- 2/92 -

HUMAN INTEREST BIO
Dave Mackay

I would like to share one other bio with you. I do this because these kind of bios were once much more prevalent in our field. They are still written from time to time by agencies representing talent, but I do not see as many of these any more as I would like. That's unfortunate because I consider these kinds of bios of great value to the client and to the media. I'm talking about long or short bios that contain refreshing quotes, revealing anecdotes and factual tell-tale human interest elements. I don't mean insider shop talk, boring generalities, flowery, but empty, phrases and exhausting superlatives.

The following bio, which I wrote some years ago, illustrates what I mean. It's about a musician, Dave Mackay, but it could be written the same way about an actor or an actress, or, for that matter, about anyone. Maybe you've written one like this. If so, I'd enjoy receiving a copy.

BIOGRAPHY: DAVE MACKAY

DAVE MACKAY'S MUSIC EXPRESSES WHAT HE
FEELS IN HIS SOUL -- BEAUTY, LOVE, JOY

Dave Mackay (it rhymes with "high") is a jazz pianist-singer-composer. He is handsome, lean, curly-haired. He is also blind. But his music is full of light.

Its appeal, he feels, is to "anyone who really loves beauty. I feel that in my soul. That, and joy!"

For a long time Mackay did not really know what kind of an effect his music had on his listeners.

"Now I know, through feedback from my audiences," he said. "I really feel my music is a healing thing."

He became aware of this while playing at the Samoa House. Recalled Mackay: "People came up to me and said, 'We come here unraveled and you make it all right again.'"

Mackay has been making it "all right again" at some of the top supper clubs in the country, including Boston's Storeyville and Jazz Workshop, New York's Left Bank and Village Vanguard, and Chicago's Mr. Kelly's. More recently he has appeared at Shelly's Manne Hole (Los Angeles), The Lighthouse (Hermosa Beach, Calif.), Donte's Jazz Supper Club (North Hollywood) and the Samoa House in Encino, Calif. , where he appeared for three years (September 1970-December 1973).

His album "Dave Mackay and Vicky Hamilton" (Impulse! AS 9184) was greeted by noted critic Rex Reed with a glowing two-column *New York Times* review, stating in part:

"Every few light years, when the moon is green and the wind seems to be blowing just the right number of knots from the west, someone comes along in the world of music and makes magic happen. Dave Mackay and Vicky Hamilton are two such people: they have knocked me on my ear. Their debut album...is far and away the best jazz thing I've heard in a long time...Mackay's piano throbs in plush Ramsay Lewis-like chords (he has a

(more)
46

phenomenal left hand)...Dave Mackay and Vicky Hamilton have revived my faith in, and nourished my hope for, music as well as art."

Mackay has performed with some of the major jazz bands of the country, including those of Bobby Hackett, Sonny Stitt, Serge Chaloff, and Charlie Mariano in Boston, and Shelly Manne, Paul Horn, Chet Baker, Don Ellis, Emil Richards, Joe Pass and Jack Sheldon in Los Angeles. He has also appeared in Los Angeles with the Hindustani Jazz Sextet.

Mackay has had co-billing with some of the jazz greats of the world, including Duke Ellington, Count Basie, Sarah Vaughan, George Shearing, Bill Evans, and Miles Davis.

His original compositions have been recorded by Cal Tjader, Emil Richards, and the Baja Marimba Band. He has appeared on two albums by Ellis and three by Richards.

While biographical statistics represent the road map of his life, the real Dave Mackay is to be found in his music and glimpses of his soul may be caught from his words: "One of the most exciting things about jazz is the deep psychic rapport that occurs among the musicians, and between musicians and listeners. Life then becomes indescribably exciting. These are the moments I try to hold on to."

Mackay considers his music a "gift" that, more than anything, serves him as "an affirmation of the basic goodness of people."

He is not out to say anything in particular with his music.

"I just try to stay close to the things I love to play and sing," he explained. "I set up structure to my music with a tremendous amount of room for the intuitive flow of new ideas. I grab onto them, become their channel, and *let* the feeling happen, rather than *make* it happen."

He has described his music as sounding "like the motions of nature." It has been said that when Mackay performs nothing seems to stand between him and the music itself.

David Owen Mackay was born in Syracuse, New York, the son of Mr. and Mrs. Donald H. Mackay, now of Hartford, Connecticut. Mackay's father sold insurance. His mother worked as a registered nurse.

"There always was music around the house," said Mackay. "My older brother, Don, was into jazz, rehearsing with his band. He had records of Art Tatum, Duke Ellington, Count Basie, Coleman Hawkins and Teddy Wilson. These are the people I was hypnotized by and went back to later. I didn't

(more)

understand a lot of it, but something within me came alive when I heard this music. I felt a sense of kinship."

He began piano lessons when he was eight years old.

"I knew I loved music enough to get up an hour-and-a-half early on cold winter mornings to practice," he said.

The family moved to Rochester, New York, and eventually to Hartford. Mackay attended school in Brighton, New York. At 15 years of age, he was sent to South Kent, an Episcopal Boys' Preparatory school.

"To all appearances I seemed like a normal child," Mackay recalled. "I started to wear glasses when I was five years old. By 12, I started to make mistakes in spatial judgments. Still, at South Kent I played football two years and rowed on the crew for four years."

He also studied piano with jazz pianist Lennie Tristano of Flushing, Long Island. Mackay began playing in small bands. When he entered Trinity College, Hartford, he was nearly blind. When he emerged, he was the first blind student to graduate from Trinity.

"I had a progressive eye disease that was not understood at the time," said Mackay. "Fortunately, I had the feeling from childhood on that I was a jazz musician and that I would be one all my life. It gave me inner security."

He earned a BA in English but continued all along with his music. At this time he met Emil Richards, who would figure significantly in his life 10 years later. He also studied with Ray Cassarino.

After Trinity, Mackay went to Boston where he met George Shearing, noted blind jazz artist, while both were working at the Storeyville Club. Shearing's advice and example helped Mackay come to grips with his blindness.

At the same time that he was appearing professionally, Mackay continued to study music for three years at Boston University and, privately, with Margaret Chaloff.

"She, musically speaking, set me on my road to freedom more than anybody," said Mackay.

That road led to appearances in the top supper clubs in the country and recognition by some of the major jazz artists of the times. Mackay defines himself musically as a "jazz pianist with roots in Art Tatum, Bud Powell and Bill Evans, coupled with an affinity for, and love of, Debussy." A baritone,

(more)

Mackay is partial vocally to the songs of Jerome Kern and considers the Sinatra of 20 years ago (the 1950s) one of his major influences.

He favors the standards of the 1940s and 1950s when performing and the bossa novas of Joabim and Joa Gilberto.

In the Sixties Mackay made contact again with Emil Richards, as both became charter members of the Hindustani Jazz Sextet, formed by Don Ellis and Hari Har Rao, and including Chuck Domanico and Steve Bohanan.

"It became a significant group, combining Indian rhythms and *ragas* (Indian scales) with modern jazz and bossa nova rhythmic feelings," explained Mackay. "We played in odd rhythms--5/4s, 7/4s, 9/4s and 7/8s. It was a very exciting time. From this came a tremendous interest in these rhythms for us and others."

The group also became part of Don Ellis Big Band, resulting in several albums.

It was the time, too, that Mackay began to compose, including five "Jaquibeaus," a kind of bossa nova in 5/4 time. His compositions, with lyrics by the late vocalist Vicky Hamilton, bear such names as "Here," "Like Me," "Now," "Peek-a-Boo," "Will-O-The-Wisp" and "See My Rainbow," some of which have been recorded by other major artists as well.

One composition, "Melissa," was inspired by his wife.

"She is a lot of things to me," said Mackay. "She has great enthusiasm and a real joy of life. She is also a good listener."

Melissa, a blonde beauty, is also a musician--a studio singer--with her "roots in classical music and heart in jazz," though ready to work in whatever musical idiom she is called upon to perform.

They were married (January 9, 1971) at the Lake Shrine of the Self-Realization Fellowship headquartered in West Los Angeles.

"It was a Hindu wedding ceremony," said Mackay. "The chapel represented all religions. It really turned me on. Friends came and played their instruments. It was so meaningful."

The two like to read, go for long walks and jog in the hills. They also are interested in metaphysics and various spiritual schools of thought and teachings.

"I spend 20 minutes twice daily in Transcendental Meditation," said Mackay. "I eat organic foods and practice yoga every day for 10 minutes. It's good for my music--and for the soul."

(more)

Sometimes as Mackay talks there are momentary hints of past turmoil. There is a feeling of still ongoing self-discovery. There, too, is an admission that he does not accept blindness heroically but that periodically he must wrestle with it before coming to grips with it again.

But above all Dave Mackay communicates a sense of wonder, openness and peace.

"I'm sitting here, smiling," he said. "I don't know what I have figured out about life but I feel I'm going in the right direction. I feel truth-oriented. Whatever it all adds up to, it's all right."

DAVE MACKAY--BIOGRAPHICAL STATISTICS

Place of birth:	Syracuse, New York
Date of birth:	March 24
Parents:	Mr. & Mrs. Donald H. Mackay of Hartford, CT
Education:	South Kent Episcopal Preparatory School, near Hartford, Connecticut; BA degree from Trinity College, Hartford, three years; Boston University, scholarship; Lennox Massachusetts School of Jazz.
Weight.	145 pounds
Height:	5'9"
Hair:	Brown
Eyes:	Hazel
Wife's name:	Melissa
Interests:	Metaphysics, Transcendental Meditation, yoga, walking, jogging

February, 1974

What you have just read is a generic biography. That means, there is no particular event that is being publicized. A bio like this can be used for a whole year, if not longer, before it needs some updating.

Δ **Structure.** One thing you don't want to do with any bio is to go chronological right away. First, you want to capture something of the essence of the person and their work. That's why a biography should have a beginning, middle and end.

Δ **First you have to create interest in the person. You also want to give the person professional credibility. That's what the beginning is all about.** See how the bio gets you quickly interested in Dave Mackay as a human being. Notice how this is done by what is first said about him and what he says himself. Capture your subject's essence and then use a quote as quickly as possible. Quotes humanize your bio.

Note also how we establish Mackay's professional credentials -- NOT through the use of glittering adjectives but by mentioning the important clubs where he has entertained and the well known performers with whom he has performed.

You can often use what other people say about your client to help paint the profile (notice how I quoted what people said who heard Mackay and what critic Rex Reed said). Why is this better than anything Mackay or I could say?

Δ **The middle part of the biography is the chronological part.** The reader should be able to tell where that starts ("David Owen Mackay was born in Syracuse, New York..."). The reason you want to go chronologically at this point is for the purpose of clarity. It's too hard to get a picture of a person's life and career if you keep jumping around.

Δ **The end.** You should end the biography with something that summarizes the person, their life, or their career. Avoid clichés. Instead, use a telling quote, a poignant fact, or a final anecdote.

What if your bio is too short (three pages instead of four) or too long (seven pages instead of six)? Maybe you need to ask a few more questions or cut what you have. If the bio must be a certain number of pages, keep working on it. If not, just let it go to its natural length.

Δ **Approval.** Be sure to submit the bio to your client for approval, before you send it out. If changes need to be made, make them. If you do not agree with the change asked for, state your reasons clearly but diplomatically. Your client, however, has final approval and the last word. That's the way it is. Also, write a long bio -- it makes your client feel more important. Keep your client happy. Remember the "e" word, "ego." In show business, particularly, it's spelled with a capital "E," regardless of claims to the contrary!

'THE SUN ALSO RISES' - PLAYERS GUIDE

JANE SEYMOUR plays Lady Brett Ashley, the sensual, desperate British aristocrat who can't have the man she really loves — so she has them all.

Born in Middlesex, England, Seymour started out as a dancer with the London Festival Ballet and switched to acting, making her film debut in "Oh What A Lovely War." This lead to roles on the stage ("Not Now Darling), a BBC dramatic series ("The Strauss Family") and the film ("Young Winston"). She played Solitaire in "Live and Let Die," and then, after two years in British repertory playing the classics, earned an Emmy nomination for her co-starring role in NBC's "Captains and the Kings." She won a Golden Globe for TV's "East of Eden," and also starred in" "The Scarlet Pimpernel," "The Dark Mirror" and "The Haunting Passion." She most recently starred in the film "Lassiter," with Tom Selleck.

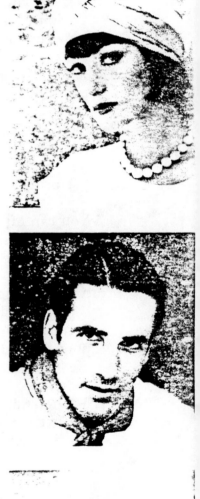

HART BOCHNER plays Jake Barnes, the young American journalist whose love for Lady Brett is frustrated by the physical and emotional wounds he suffered in World War I.

Bochner, son of actor Lloyd Bochner, broke into films in Hemingway's 1976 "Islands in the Stream." In 1979 he appeared as a snobbish fraternity brother in the hit film "Breaking Away." His television work includes "East of Eden," "Haywire" and "Having it All." Other film credits include playing Jaqueline Bisset's lover in "Rich and Famous" and upcoming roles as the heroine's romantic interest in "Supergirl" and a policeman in "The Wild Life."

LEONARD NIMOY plays The Count, the eccentric Russian emigre who is fascinated by Lady Brett and refuses to be cast aside when she is through with him.

Famous around the world for his portrayal of Spock in the "Star Trek" TV and film series, Nimoy was born in Boston and got his start in such 1950's films as "Francis Gors To West Point" and "The Overland Trail." His other features include "Deathwatch" and "The Balcony." After TV's "Star Trek," Nimoy co-starred for two years on "Mission: Impossible" and then on the stage in such plays as "Fiddler on the Roof" and "One Flew Over the Cuckoo's Nest.". In between such miniseries as NBC's "Marco Polo" and "Golda," Nimoy directed episodes of "T. J. Hooker," "The Powers of Matthew Star," and his one-man stage show "Vincent." He recently directed the feature "Star Trek III: The Search For Spock."

IAN CHARLESON plays Mike Campbell, the carousing, Scottish war hero who is engaged to Lady Brett but knows he can never really win her heart from Jake Barnes.

Best-known for his role as Eric Liddel, the devout Scottish runner in "Chariots of Fire," Charleson was born in Scotland and appeared on the British stage in such plays as "Joseph and the Amazing Technicolor Dreamcoat," "Much Ado About Nothing," "Look Back in Anger." Recently, Charleson co-starred in the Oscar-winning "Ghandi" and on television in the "Master of the Game" miniseries.

ROBERT CARRADINE plays Robert Cohn, the Jewish-American writer — and amateur boxer — who expresses his emotions better with his fists than with his pen.

Born into an acting family, Carradine recently starred in "Revenge of the Nerds." He made his film debut opposite John Wayne in "The Cowboys" and was also featured in the films "Coming Home," "The Big Red One," "The Long Riders," "Heartaches," "Mean Streets," and "Aloha Bobby and Rose." A musician since age nine, he regularly plays guitar at Southern California clubs. In addition, he races Corvettes for Goodyear and Guldstrand and his team recently won the 24-hour Nelson Ledges race.

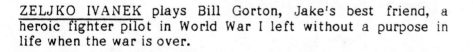

ZELJKO IVANEK plays Bill Gorton, Jake's best friend, a heroic fighter pilot in World War I left without a purpose in life when the war is over.

Soon to be seen co-starring with Jack Lemmon in the film, "Mass Appeal," Zeljko was born in Yugoslavia and studied drama at Yale. He appeared on the New York stage in "The Survivor" and "Cloud 9" and received a Tony nomination for Best Supporting Actor for his performance in Neil Simon's "Brighton Beach Memoirs." He made his film debut in "Tex" and starred in the psychological thriller "The Sender."

(more)

STEPHANE AUDRAN plays Georgette, an aging prostitute who befriends Jake Barnes and takes him on a tour of shady nightspots in Paris.

Audran, born in Versailles, France, made her acting debut on the Paris stage. She first collaborated with director Claude Chabrol on "Les Cousins" and went on to make 15 more films with him including "Les Biches," "Violette Noziere" and "La Femme Infidele." Her English language films include "The Black Bird," "The Silver Bears" and "The Big Red One."

ANDREA OCCHIPINTI plays Pedro Romero, a young and passionate bullfighter, inexperienced in romance, who falls in love with Lady Brett.

Occhipinti was recently seen in another bullfighting role as Bo Derek's lover in "Bolero." Born in Rome and educated in London, Occhipinti has been seen by American audiences in the PBS miniseries "The Chart House of Parma" and the film "Innocents Abroad."

————o————

November, 1984
#1220Y

'THE SUN ALSO RISES' PRODUCTION TEAM

JOHN FURIA
Executive Producer

Furia, under his banner of Furia/Oringer Productions, was executive producer of NBC-TV's high-rated miniseries, "Sidney Sheldon's Rage of Angels" and several TV movies including "The Intruder Within," "The Hustler of Muscle Beach" and "The Death of Ocean View Park." He produced the TV movies "The Widow," "The Healers" and the pilot film for "The Blue Knight." His series production credits include "Kung-Fu," "John O'Hara's Gibbsville" and "Apple's Way." His writing credits include the feature, "The Singing Nun," and episodes of "Dupont Show of the Month," "Chrysler Theatre," "Twilight Zone," "Dr. Kildare" and "The Waltons." He has also produced nearly one hundred television dramas for the public service series, "Insight."

ROBERT L. JOSEPH
Producer/Writer

Joseph, who wrote the miniseries "The Word," and NBC's "World War III" and "Sidney Sheldon's Rage of Angels," began his show business career by producing a string of successful Broadway plays, including "The Father," "Tiger At the Gates," and Shaw's "Major Barbara" and "Heartbreak House." As a playwright, Joseph's credits include "Face of A Hero," which first appeared as a Playhouse 90 production on TV and "The Isle of Children." His feature films are "The Third Secret," "Echoes of Summer," and "Companions In Nightmare." During television's Golden Age, he wrote "Face of a Hero," "In Darkness Waiting" for Kraft Theatre, "Memorandum For A Spy" for Chrysler Theatre and "Footnote To Fame" for Westinghouse Playhouse. He also wrote the TV movies "Dr. Max" and "Death Flight" and is about to start work on a "Rage of Angles: The Story Continues" for NBC.

JAMES GOLDSTONE
Director

Goldstone won an Emmy Award for the NBC-TV's "Kent State" and an Emmy nomination for "A Clear and Present Danger." His theatrical features include "Winning," "Red Sky At Morning," "Rollercoaster" and "Swashbuckler." He directed the TV pilots of "Star Trek" and "Ironsides" as well as the TV movies, "Calamity Jane," "Charles and Diana," "Studs Lonigan," "Eric," "Things in Their Season," "Cry Panic," "Doctor Max," "Journey From Darkness," and "Shadow Over Elveron." He began his directing career on such TV series as "Bat Masterson," Dr. Kildare," "Chrysler Theatre," "The Fugitive," "Eleventh Hour" and "Route 66."

---o---

SARAH, PLAIN AND TALL

BIOGRAPHIES

GLENN CLOSE (Executive Producer/Sarah Wheaton) was born in Greenwich, Connecticut, the daughter of a surgeon. After studying acting at William and Mary College, she made her professional stage debut on Broadway, appearing in a repertory season with the Phoenix Theatre Company. Close received her first Tony nomination while starring in "Barnum," and was spotted by director George Roy Hill, who cast her in "The World According To Garp." Her performance as Jenny Fields earned her the first of three Academy Award nominations as Best Supporting Actress; the others were for "The Big Chill" and "The Natural." Glenn Close received Best Actress Academy Award nominations for "Fatal Attraction" (1987) and "Dangerous Liaisons" (1988). Recent films include "Reversal of Fortune," with Jeremy Irons, and "Hamlet," with Mel Gibson. Close appeared on television in the 1988 HALLMARK HALL OF FAME presentation of "Stones For Ibarra," based on the Harriet Doerr novel.

# # #

CHRISTOPHER WALKEN (Jacob Witting) was born in the New York borough of Queens. He's been performing since the age of 10, when he joined his two brothers on live television shows in the 1950s. Walken made his Broadway debut in the musicals "High Spirits" and "Baker Street." Switching to drama, he soon amassed such prestigious theatrical prizes as an Obie for "Kid Champion," a Theatre World Award for "The Rose Tattoo" and the Clarence Derwent Award for "The Lion in Winter." More recent stage triumphs include David Rabe's "Hurlyburly" and John Guare's "The House of Blue Leaves." Walken appeared on television in the 1966 HALLMARK HALL OF FAME presentation of "Barefoot in Athens."

Christopher Walken's feature films include "The Anderson Tapes," "Next Stop, Greenwich Village," "Roseland," "Annie Hall" and "The Deer Hunter." His performance in the latter earned the actor an Academy Award as Best Supporting Actor of 1979. Subsequent motion pictures include "Pennies from Heaven," "Heaven's Gate," "The Milagro Beanfield War," "Biloxi Blues" and "King of New York."

# # #

Hallmark
Hall of Fame

CHRISTOPHER BELL (Caleb Witting) is six years old; he's in grade one at St. Paul's Weaver Elementary School. This is the first time he's been on television. He earned his first professional credit at Minneapolis' Guthrie Theatre, in a production of "The Duchess of Malfi." In 1989, in the same theater, he played "Tiny Tim" in "A Christmas Carol." The Bell family (which includes four boys and one girl) loves animals; they have five cats and three dogs.

# # #

LEXI RANDALL (Anna Witting) is a grade five student in Houston, Texas. After her daughter won four oratory contests, Mrs. Randall enrolled Lexi in an acting school. Her teacher at the school recommended her for a part in the latest Whoopi Goldberg film, "Long Walk Home" (in which she plays Sissy Spacek's daughter). Lexi Randall is an inveterate doll collector, an avid Girl Scout and an active member of her church. She is also a straight-A student.

# # #

JON DE VRIES (Matthew Grant) appeared most recently in the New York Shakespeare Festival production of "Titus Andronicus." He has appeared on Broadway in "Major Barbara," "Loose Ends" and "The Cherry Orchard." Off-Broadway credits include "The Ballad of Soapy Smith," "Agamemnon" and the La MaMa ETC. production of "Fragments of a Trilogy," which has toured all over the world. Television work includes movies ("Too Young the Hero"), miniseries ("Lincoln") and series ("In the Heat of the Night" and "The Young Riders"). Feature films include "First Deadly Sin" and "Fatman and Little Boy."

# # #

MARGARET SOPHIE STEIN (Maggie Grant) has worked extensively in television in Poland, where her credits include "The Trip to the Happiness" and "Crime and Punishment." On the stage in this country her work includes leading roles in productions of "Don Juan," "The Decameron," "Karamazov Brothers" and "School of Wives." Her feature films include Andrzej Wadja's "Danton" and Paul Mazursky's "Enemies, A Love Story."

# # #

GLENN JORDAN (Producer/Director) began his career in the theater, where his direction credits included "A Streetcar Named Desire," "Rosencrantz and Guildenstern Are Dead" and "The Glass Menagerie." For his work in television he has received five Emmy awards. He has produced and/or directed "Heartsounds," "The Women's Room," "Les Miserables," "In the Matter of Karen Ann Quinlan," "Echoes in the Darkness," "Dress Grey" and "Challenger." Previous HALLMARK HALL OF FAME credits are "The Court Martial of George Armstrong Custer" (1977), "Home Fires Burning" (1989) and "Promise" (1986), for which he won an Emmy for best direction; the picture won a total of five Emmys. Glenn Jordan's film credits include "Only When I Laugh," which received three Academy Award nominations, "The Buddy System" and "Mass Appeal."

# # #

PATRICIA MacLACHLAN (Author/Screenwriter) was born in Cheyenne, Wyoming. A graduate of the University of Connecticut, she is a frequent lecturer on the subject of children's literature, and has conducted workshops at several universities and colleges. MacLachlan is the author of several picture books and three novels: Arthur, For the Very First Time, Cassie Binegar and Unclaimed Treasures. Her book Sarah, Plain and Tall is based on a true event in her family history. It was awarded the prestigious Newbery Medal for outstanding children's literature in 1986.

# # #

EDWIN SELF (Supervising Producer) began his television career as associate producer of the "Lancer" series; he subsequently produced the "Emergency" and "Code R" series. Edwin Self's television films include "Uncommon Valor," "Broken Vows," "Spies, Lies and Naked Thighs" and "Incident at Lincoln Bluff." His most recent telefilm was the Emmy-winning "The Incident," starring Walter Matthau.

# # #

WILLIAM SELF (Executive Producer) has over 30 years of production experience in the television industry. One of the first programs he produced was "The Frank Sinatra Show." He went on to help create the immensely popular and highly-acclaimed "Twilight Zone," "Batman" and "M*A*S*H" series. As president of CBS Theatrical Films, Self oversaw the production of several features, including "The Lightship," "Target," "Eleni" and "Better Off Dead." He was a co-executive producer on the HALLMARK HALL OF FAME production of "The Tenth Man."

# # #

Press Contacts:

Stone/Hallinan Associates, Inc.
Los Angeles: 213/655-8970
New York: 212/489-5590

Hallmark Cards
Television Programming
816/274-8099

30 Rockefeller Plaza
New York, NY 10112
212 664-4444

Media Relations
National Broadcasting
Company, Inc.

NBC
BIOGRAPHY

TED DANSON

Sam Malone in 'Cheers'

Thursdays (9–9:30 p.m. NYT) on NBC-TV

Ted Danson has received four consecutive Emmy Award nominations for his portrayal of Sam Malone. He's also been able to pursue an active and successful career in feature films and television movies. During a hiatus from "Cheers" production this year, he traveled to Africa to co-produce and star in the TV movie "We Are the Children," which sheds light on that country's devastating famine. When not working, he spends a great deal of time supporting community organizations such as Futures for Children, an American Indian self-help program.

Danson was born in San Diego and raised in Flagstaff, AZ, where he grew up with Hopi and Navajo children. He attended Stanford University, discovered drama, and transferred to Carnegie Tech to pursue that field.

His first job in New York City was in the Off-Broadway play "The Real Inspector Hound," which eventually was presented at the Kennedy Center in Washington, DC. Danson progressed to Shakespeare-in-the-Park, commercials, and the NBC daytime dramas "The Doctors" and "Somerset."

In 1978 he and his bride, environmental designer Casey Coates, moved to Los Angeles and managed the Actors Institute for 18 months while he taught there. He landed the role of Ian Campbell in the film "The Onion Field," before getting guest roles in such TV series as "Laverne and Shirley," "Family" and "Magnum P.I." He co-starred in the TV movie "The Women's Room," and in the feature films "Body Heat," "Little Treasure," "A Fine Mess" and "Just Between Friends." He recently co-starred with Tom Selleck and Steve Guttenberg in the upcoming feature film "Three Men and a Baby."

Danson was awarded a Golden Globe for his performance in the TV movie "Something About Amelia," and last year he made his debut as a producer via the NBC movie "When the Bough Breaks," in which he also starred.

BIOGRAPHICAL SUMMARY — TED DANSON

Birthplace/birthdate:	San Diego, CA/December 29
Height/weight:	6'2"/180 lbs.
Color hair/eyes:	Brown/blue
Family:	Married, wife's name Casey; daughters Kate (7) and Alexis (3)
Residence:	Los Angeles, CA

———o———   Fall, 1987

BIOGRAPHY
_____

TIMOTHY DALY
as Joe Hackett

Timothy Daly stars as straitlaced good-guy Joe Hackett, pilot and owner of fledgling commuter airline Sandpiper Air, in Paramount Network Television's "Wings" on NBC-TV. Daly first came to national attention in 1982 when he starred as Billy, the friend home from graduate school, in Barry Levinson's hit film "Diner." During the 1988-89 television season, he was seen in the starring role of Norman Foley in CBS-TV's acclaimed series "Almost Grown." He also won rave reviews and a Theatre World Award for his role as a lifeguard in the 1987 Tony-nominated Broadway hit "Coastal Disturbances."

Daly grew up in Suffern, New York, the son of actors James ("Medical Center") and Hope Daly. Both Tim and sister Tyne ("Cagney and Lacey") caught the acting bug at an early age, and after performing in numerous high school plays, Tim majored in Drama at Bennington College. He won his first professional role while still in school in a summer stock production of "Equus," and headed for New York after graduation to study acting and singing. Only a year and a half later, in 1982, he was cast as Billy in "Diner."

Daly went on to perform frequently with the Trinity Square Repertory Theater in Providence, Rhode Island, where he met his wife, actress Amy Van Nostrand. His many regional theater credits include "Mass Appeal" and "Bus Stop" at the Trinity Square, "A Knife In The Heart" at the Williamstown Playhouse, and a starring role opposite Amy Irving in "The Glass Menagerie" at the Santa Fe Festival Theater.

Grub Street Productions
in association with

(more...)

A Paramount Communications Company

61

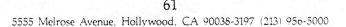

On television, Daly appeared opposite Tom Hulce in the American Playhouse Production of "The Rise and Rise of Daniel Rocket," and starred with Valerie Bertinelli in the miniseries "I'll Take Manhattan." He also starred in the NBC-TV movie "Mirrors" and in the telefilm "Red Earth, White Earth," and was a series regular in both "Ryan's Four" and "Almost Grown." Among his additional feature film credits are "Made In Heaven," "Love Or Money" and "Just The Way You Are."

Daly is an accomplished guitarist who also writes music, and enjoys all sports, particularly baseball. He and Amy Van Nostrand are the parents of two young children, Sam and Emelyn, and make their permanent home in Providence, Rhode Island.

#   #   #

CONTACTS: Leah Krantzler 213/965-1990
              Marisa Spitz 212/986-7080
              THE LIPPIN GROUP

              John A. Wentworth 213/956-5394
              V.P., Ad./Pub./Promo.
              Network Television Division
              PARAMOUNT PICTURES

4

FEATURES

There is a difference of opinion these days about the value of feature stories. Time was when editors would take feature stories -- especially if they were sent to them on an exclusive basis in their area -- and run these on their TV pages and in their Sunday TV supplements.

Often a 500-word feature story (two pages, double spaced) would be printed in full. At other times the stories were used in part.

For five years, in fact, I was the feature writer in the NBC Press Department on the West Coast, and we sent out two features a week on an exclusive basis to newspapers in over 130 cities.

Why have newspapers cut down on the use of such features? One reason is lack of space. There's too much television news that must be covered to allow for 500-word features. Furthermore, TV editors have become much more critical about what goes into their TV pages and TV supplements. They are more issue-oriented now; they prefer staff-written analytical pieces; they exercise much more control over content; and they tend to use staff-written mini-features, in order to cover the many more shows now available on the many more channels.

THEIR VALUE Still there's something to be said for including features in TV press kits. Like bios, which don't get published, features can serve a useful purpose. They suggest interview angles; they provide background; they can arouse interest in a star and in a show. Furthermore, if an editor decides to talk to a star and do a story on a particular show, the editor may still take parts of your feature and work them into his or her story. Or an editor may use part of your feature for one or more column items.

HOW MANY TO WRITE How many features should you write? That depends. If you are publicizing a series, you may send out features periodically on an on-going basis. If you're publicizing a TV special, TV-movie, or miniseries you may want to generate two, four or even more features for your press kit. What you do depends on a number of factors: 1) The number of stars in your show (if you have many major stars, you can have a field day); 2) The politics of the situation (if you have four stars who have equal billing, it may be advisable to do a feature on each one of them; 3) Budget considerations -- if you have to keep your press kit down to a certain number of pages, it may be best to write a few pages of production notes and items, which can cover more ground than than features; and 4) Whether you can find enough feature material to write about.

STRUCTURE

Δ **A feature deals with one particular theme.** It, too, has a beginning, middle and end. It shares many of the qualities of a biography, when it comes to style:

- A punchy lead that fascinates, provokes, amuses, or intrigues the reader
- Short words, short sentences, short paragraphs
- Quotes alternating with transitional sentences
- Reference in the second, third or fourth paragraph to what makes the story newsworthy and topical (the show you are publicizing)

Δ **Finding the angle.** You can usually find the angle for a feature by thinking about the role and what the actor is required to do. Ask yourself, if you were playing that role, what would you wonder about? What would you want to know? What would intrigue you? What would scare you? What about makeup, wardrobe, location, hardships? Other questions to ask the actor: Have you ever played this kind of role before? When? What is the most opposite role to this one that you have played? What was your favorite role? What would you like to play? Why? How does this role relate to you personally? This story? Have you worked with any of the other actors before? When and in what capacity? How did you get this role? Has anything unusual happened on the set? What do you think of the story, the theme?

You may think of additional, personal questions to ask. Before you talk with the talent, read their biography and any newspaper or magazine clippings. These may suggest other questions.

EXAMPLES Note how differently **Hart Bochner** and **Jane Seymour** approached their roles in **NBC-TV's "The Sun Also Rises,"** based on Ernest Hemingway's famous novel. As a result, you have two fascinating feature stories.

Δ **Celebrity features.** What else, besides stars, will interest the media? Realistically, very little else. Remember that the media are highly competitive. Print media want to attract readers and broadcast media want to attract viewers. That means stars, superstars and megastars -- the bigger the better. So you should keep that in mind in the features you do. Whether that's the way it should be or not, is another matter. But that's the reality.

Δ **Non-celebrity features.** Still there are other features that can get you attention and publicity. Take a look, for instance, at the feature on **screenwriter Robert L. Joseph,** who adapted Hemingway's novel to television.

Joseph is not a recognizable on-screen personality like Bochner or Seymour. Few writers have celebrity status, where their name is as recognizable as that of the major Hollywood TV and motion picture stars. However, here is a heavy-duty writer ("World War III" and "Rage of Angels") working on a Hemingway project. Hemingway thus provides the celebrity status which the media might find of interest. The fact that Joseph had met Hemingway and was something of an authority on his work strengthens the angle and the story. Being writers themselves, print media journalists probably found this feature of particular interest, most likely leading to a desire to do something on the miniseries, even if they did not use this feature itself.

HART BOCHNER FELT A 'RESPONSIBILITY' PLAYING HEMINGWAY HERO

Portraying a fictional hero is a common challenge for an actor. But for Hart Bochner, playing Jake Barnes in NBC-TV's "The Sun Also Rises" was downright risky.

"I was not just playing Jake Barnes, I was trying to be true to the Hemingway mystique," Bochner says. "This is the biggest professional responsibility I've ever had because millions of people have read the novel and have their own ideas about how the character should dress, stand, talk and move."

Accepting that "responsibility," Bochner did a thorough analysis of what made Jake Barnes tick.

"Jake is a victim of World War I — the war to end all wars. He lost his manhood in an explosion. He now lives in Paris as a journalist but I don't think that 'living' is exactly the right word. He goes through the motions of life without really living it. But he has no self-pity about his physical and emotional situation. He just gets on with things."

Bochner says Barnes, like the other main characters in the NBC miniseries, Sunday and Monday, Dec. 9 and 10 (9-11 p.m. NYT each night), are emotionally scarred by the ravages of World War I.

"Their psyches are still in the trenches," he says. "Although Jake is a calming influence on his friends, when he's alone at night and no longer absorbed by their problems, his own demons come out to haunt him."

Bochner says Jake's "reserve" was the biggest hurdle in playing the part.

"Much of his dialogue is sparse and he reveals little of what is going on inside him," Bochner says. "Jake is a very controlled person. I had to somehow let the audience know the inner hell this man is going through.

"His greatest torment," Bochner continues, "is Lady Brett Ashley (played by Jane Seymour). Here is this beautiful, exotic woman he has fallen in love with, but knows he can never really have. That's what makes their romance so intense."

—o—

November, 1984
#1217Y

Press Department/3000 W. Alameda Ave./Burbank, CA 91523

JANE SEYMOUR 'HAD TO' PLAY THE COMPLEX LADY BRETT

At the time Jane Seymour was approached to play the beautiful Lady Brett Ashley in NBC-TV's "The Sun Also Rises," she also had offers for three different film roles. But after reading the script for the four-hour miniseries based on Ernest Hemingway's classic novel, she knew there was only one choice to make.

"The character of Lady Brett simply got inside me and I HAD to do it," says Seymour, who stars with Hart Bochner and Leonard Nimoy in the two-part drama to be telecast Sunday and Monday, Dec. 9 and 10 (9-11 p.m. NYT each night).

"The first thing I did was read 'Hemingway's Women,' a nonfiction work about his life and times. Most interesting to me were the sections on Lady Duff Twysden, the woman on whom Brett is supposedly based. I wanted to know all about Brett's background and by reading about Lady Duff, I was able to flesh out my character's history."

But how does one actually play a character etched in the minds of the millions who have read the novel?

"There are hundreds of different ways to play such a complex character," Seymour says. "The choices are infinite because she is several women in one — she is so difficult to explain. Therefore, I had to go by my own instincts.

"I love Brett's spirit and strength. There are a few men in the piece who are actually dependent upon her. And she is able to make those men feel very special, perhaps even loved, even though she doesn't really love them. She seems drawn towards needy men with problems and they in turn are drawn to her because she is able to make them feel loved.

"Jake Barnes (Bochner), the man she really loves, she can't have because he was left impotent by a war wound. She is so complex it's possible that had he been healthy, she would have lost interest in him.

"She's like some life-risking trapeze artist who swings from man to man. Jake is under her like some safety net that picks up the pieces when she gets herself into a messy situation."

(more)

Seymour says the toughest part of playing Brett was the need to often project two or more emotions at once.

"For instance, there's a scene where I dance a mad Charleston on a nightclub table and I am surrounded by handsome adoring men. I look like the epitome of joyousness but actually I'm coming apart at the seams.

"Essentially," she continues, "this is a classy woman who is really drunk half of the time but never shows it. Even when someone attempts to kill her, the first thing she says is ' this is the most vulgar thing I've ever heard of!

"How could an actress not adore a part like that?"

——o——

November, 1984
#1216Y

SCREENWRITER WROTE 'THE SUN ALSO RISES'
LIKE ERNEST HEMINGWAY MIGHT HAVE DONE IT

Why adapt Ernest Hemingway's classic novel "The Sun Also Rises" into a television miniseries?

"Why not?" says Robert L. Joseph, the writer/producer of NBC-TV's "The Sun Also Rises," <u>Sunday and Monday, Dec. 9 and 10</u> (9-11 p.m. NYT each night). "Why not give millions of people, who have never been exposed to Hemingway, a taste of his work."

"Usually the purists get all riled up when a classic of this sort is done in another medium," Joseph says, "but I want to stress that I'm ADAPTING the novel, not CHANGING it — and there's a big difference. I've taken an impressionistic piece and I'm trying to make it work in another medium. I've read all of Hemingway and I tried to write my screenplay as he would have written it."

Joseph, the talented writer of such NBC miniseries as "World War III" and Sidney Sheldon's "Rage of Angels," is no stranger to Hemingway. He met the famed author several times during the 1950's and is somewhat of an authority on his work.

"'The Sun Also Rises' is by far Hemingway's best book," Joseph says. "It's not only one of the greatest love stories ever written it's also one of the greatest anti-war novels of our time. It's a work about the biggest and most devastating of all wars — World War I. That's the war that took unsophisticated youths off farms and out of small towns and threw them face-to-face with grenades, bombs, and lethal gas. Millions died and the male populations of the countries of Europe have never been the same.

"But there was another kind of wound just as catastrophic as a physical one and that was the psychological wounding of the millions of young men who emerged from the war, dead in spirit. They comprised the generation of the twenties that we referred to as 'sheiks' and 'mad youth.' These were the young people who lived madly for the moment, intensely trying to recapture the innocence and feelings they'd lost. These are the characters of 'The Sun Also Rises.'

(more)

69

The major challenge for Joseph was to turn an impressionistic novel into four hours of dramatically compelling television.

"To make the piece more linear, I enlarged the part of The Count, played by Leonard Nimoy. He is much more prominent in the miniseries than the novel. He is the hook at the end of the first part that will make viewers stay tuned. He is the man who finally shows Lady Brett (Jane Seymour) she cannot toy so loosely with the affections of men.

"I know there will be critics and viewers out there who will chastise me for touching Hemingway, but I cannot agree with them. If those people were truly right, it would mean that we'd never adapt any novel into another form.

"Even though it has sold over five million copies, 'The Sun Also Rises' deserves an even wider audience. Somebody had to take on that challenge."

————o————

November, 1984
#1223Y

5

STORYLINES
&
FORMAT STORIES

The terms "storyline" and "format story" are sometimes used interchangeably. Strictly speaking, **"storyline"** refers to a **brief description** of a TV program or weekly episode of a TV series and **"format story"** refers to a **full program description** of a TV series, special, variety program, TV movie, or other form of TV presentation.

Δ **Basic purpose.** A storyline has one basic purpose: to give an editor a capsulized version of program, so the editor may use it for the log listing or when writing about, or reviewing, the show.

A format story is fuller than a storyline and contains within it the elements of a storyline. It may also contain information about the stars, the production team, and the production itself, as well as future shows.

STORYLINES

To write a storyline you need the following:
√   A final script (When you cover a show, you must ask for a script and all page revisions; don't ever trust the original script; it may change radically)
√   Opening titles and closing credits (These will tell you how the actors are billed; if the credits are not ready when you write your storyline, make sure you get accurate information -- correct billing information and correct spelling of names -- from a reliable and responsible source)
√   Cast list (This is available at the start of production)
√   Crew list (This gives you the names of the production team)
√   Other (Sometimes there is a show description or synopsis available)

Time was when networks devoted a full page to episodic storylines. No more. The storylines have been cut to the bone. That's the way log listings are and the storylines are intended to service the log writers. Furthermore, few editors write about weekly episodes, so they don't need more information. If there is ever anything special about a weekly episode, it can be given special handling.

Δ **State the Conflict.** There is an art to writing brief storylines. In short, you must be able to state the main conflict. Keep that in mind when you read the script. Ask yourself, "What's the basic conflict in this story?" and then try to state it in the fewest words possible. You must take the concrete details and reduce these to their essence. Don't tell the whole story. State the conflict.

"Homefront"   Look at the storyline for the "Patriots" episode of the "Homefront" series. What's the conflict? A husband and wife are at odds over their foreign-born daughter-in-law -- the wife wants her deported, but her husband has personal reasons for wanting his daughter-in-law to stay. Conflict! That's what drama is all about. The point of the storyline is to get the viewer to watch your show -- you arouse his interest through a statement of the conflict and the inherent question, "How will this issue get resolved?"

Δ **Since a series has regular stars, it is essential to always involve the main stars in your storyline.** Remember, the viewers tune in from week to week to find out what situations the lead characters are going to be involved with this time. Even if there is a major guest star, you must still build your storyline around your lead characters. Notice how this is done here. The storyline talks about Ruth, Gina and Mike Sloan.

Δ **Study your client's format carefully.** You must use that same format every time. Don't get "creative" with storylines. They are meant to be functional and to convey basic information succinctly. Editors look for consistency here. Don't confuse editors by changing the way you write your storyline every week. If you analyze one storyline, you should be able to figure out how to write all upcoming storylines for that series and for other, similar series. Analyze everything -- from the contents of each paragraph to the way the show information is handled. Every punctuation mark matters -- so follow the established style!   .

Here's what you can tell from studying this particular storyline:

- ENTERTAINMENT letterhead
- Release date above the headline, to the left
- Headline, bold-face and all caps, centered; name of series in double-quotes (some styles call for single quotes in headlines and double quotes in the body of the story)
- First paragraph
  -- Name of episode in caps/lower case, double quotes, followed by a double hyphen (--)
  -- Use character names only
  -- State conflict in one or two sentences
  -- Name of series in caps/lower, case, double quotes
  -- Day, month, date bold-faced, capitalized

        -- Time in parentheses, 10:00, not 10 p.m., lower case, ET for
            Eastern Time, comma after last parenthesis
        -- End paragraph with: on the ABC Television Network

- Second paragraph: names of actors and the characters they play (in correct billing order)
- Third paragraph: names of guest stars and the characters they play
- Release is single-spaced, with a space between paragraphs
- Sign off with **-- ABC --** in bold-face

"Civil Wars" Now take a look at the "Daveja Vu All Over Again" storyline for the "Civil Wars" series. Note how this, too, follows the same format in every detail but one: the first paragraph mentions three conflicts, rather than just one. Why is that? Probably because that show is structured differently dramatically. Instead of one main plot, you have several plots. State your conflict as succinctly as possible. Count the number of words in each of the three plot descriptions here -- each description has captured the conflict and boiled it down to the bare bones. This doesn't happen automatically. You must work with your words until they say exactly what you want them to say succinctly! Semi-colons are good for separating several themes.

The second and third paragraph provide an interesting variation from the other storylines we looked at. In reading these paragraphs, there is no question about who the regular stars of the series are and who the guest stars are in this episode. Which of the two approaches do you prefer? Why?

"Doctor, Doctor" CBS handles its storylines a bit differently. Take a look at the "Doctor, Doctor" episode. What do you notice about:

- The series title -- how it is written and punctuated?
- The statement of conflict?
- The way the day, month and date are spelled and punctuated?
- The way the time is listed (there are two differences here from the ABC style; one is the use of ET/PT; PT means Pacific Time); what else is different here?

CBS lists the name of the director and writer in its storylines. Find the reference. CBS uses a second paragraph to expand on the storyline. How can you tell what episode this is?

CBS provides the names of the actors and characters by providing a cast list. This list follows the billing order. That's helpful to an editor who may want to run only a few names in the log listing because of limited space. He may wonder if there is a guest star who should be listed. By looking at the second paragraph, he can tell that Ann Marie Lee is a guest star and should be mentioned.

If a program provides a special service to its viewers, be sure and mention it. See the box underneath the cast list. The storyline ends with three centered stars (* * *) rather than the network call letters.

"Evening Shade"   There are a number of interesting elements about the "Evening Shade" episode. We are informed that this is a rebroadcast of the premiere episode. Note how this is mentioned in the headline, the body of the first paragraph, and again at the end of the first paragraph where the date of the original broadcast is given parenthetically).

This time, when the writer is listed, we are given additional, important information, namely, that the writer is also the creator and executive producer of the series.

When a show preempts another show, that information must be mentioned.

This storyline is longer than most episodic storylines (instead of two paragraphs, it is three paragraphs long). What accounts for this is that it was the premiere episode featuring many major stars.

STORYLINES FOR MINISERIES   Miniseries come in all shapes and sizes. Some run consecutively for two or more nights. Others run weekly, for a limited period of time. However they're broken up, you should provide storylines for each night the show airs. This can be done in one release or separate releases. If you don't do this, you will only get a generic log listing, which says the same thing every night. Such listings can be misleading. A viewer may think it's a repeat of something he has seen already. Or it may lead to confusion (which night of the miniseries is this?). But worst of all, it can lead to channel switching if there is nothing new to grab the viewer's attention. It can also lead to irritation. A miniseries features many stars, but they may not all be seen every night. Viewers don't want to miss their favorite stars. You want to make sure that they are listed the night they are appearing. The listings may also attract new viewers. Finally, editors are likely to give more space to a miniseries when they have something new and different to report for each evening.

"Brideshead Revisited"   "Brideshead Revisited" was an 11-part series which aired Monday nights on PBS under the umbrella title of "Great Performances." Take a look at the storyline for the fourth episode, "Sebastian Against the World." It has an entirely different look from the ones we have studied so far. However, this look remains consistent for all 11 storylines for the series. If you had to take over and write the remaining seven storylines, you could do so easily by analyzing this one and following its format. The basic elements that go into the writing of a storyline are still there. They have just been rearranged.

Read the first paragraph. Is there conflict? Yes. This storyline, however, goes on for four paragraphs. It reveals more of the plot, capturing the continuous conflict. The stars here are listed parenthetically as the characters are introduced in the body of the narrative. When writing this kind of storyline, it's important that you make a list of the stars who must be mentioned. If it's necessary to list them in a particular order, make sure you know that order. Then create the storyline around your stars. Don't get sidetracked with secondary roles and story material. If that happens, stop, rethink and rewrite the storyline.

SUGGESTED HIGHLIGHT LISTING Here's something we haven't seen before, a SUGGESTED HIGHLIGHT LISTING which you will find on the second page of this storyline. You will find this on most storylines involving TV-movies, specials, variety programs, and other event presentations. This is the whole show in a nutshell. It is what you would like to see in a log listing or "recommended viewing" listing. By preparing such a highlight, you are helping the editor. You are also making sure that what you and your client consider essential has a good chance of getting into such a listing. If you don't do this, names that should be listed often get left out and show descriptions can get messed up. This can happen still, but at least you're off the hook, if you have provided a good program highlight.

Δ **Finally there is the "boiler plate" paragraph.** That's the last paragraph that contains information that you are required to provide each time you send out a release. It usually has something to do with the various parties that need to be credited in the production of a program.

Δ **Media contact.** Press releases often have more than one media contact. This release lists the PR agency responsible for the preparation of the press kit and media campaign and the PBS station involved in the production and media campaign.

FORMAT STORIES I have included this format story as much for style as for structure. As far as structure is concerned, you have here 1) a description of what the series is about (synopsis), 2) executive **"Fantastic Max"** producer and producer credits, and 3) cast list (voices). As you read the description of the series, you should immediately become aware of a major difference between this kind of writing and the writing we have seen so far in storylines and format stories. The writing here is playful, descriptive, colorful. It is much closer to promotional writing than journalistic writing. So why's it done here, and even allowed here? The answer is: animation. We're in a different reality. This is fantasy. So the language becomes much more fanciful. This release happens to be from Hanna-Barbera Productions. But if you look at a Disney release, or one from DIC Enterprises or Film Roman, you will find that they share this style in common. If you're in the habit of writing journalistically, you will have to let yourself go more when writing this kind of publicity material. It may take a few attempts until you get the feel of it.

"Cheers"   Here we have a one-page, double-spaced format story
                      from NBC. It is kept to a single page because it goes into
the network press kit, which contains information on every show airing in all dayparts (daytime, primetime, late-night) on the network. That's a lot of shows and that's why network press releases are kept brief. The other consideration, besides space, is cost. The size of the network press kit could easily double, if you did not put length restrictions on each release, whether it's a format story, biography, or credit sheet.

"Cheers," at this point, is not a new series but a returning series. Just as you do with the bios of the returning stars, you want to update the information about the series. How successful was the series in the last season in terms of awards or ratings? How successful has it been since it premiered? What's new about the series? This format story offers a good generic description of the series and of the cast regulars. Note how the stars are listed parenthetically. The release concludes with such essentials as the name(s) of the production company(ies), executive producer(s), producer(s), director, and, where appropriate, writer(s).

Notice that the broadcast information (day, time, and network) is part of the head. The one piece of information not listed is the premiere date for the new season. Often these format stories are released before a date has been set. The date must then be announced in a separate release.

"The Sun   Actually, we have two format stories here. One, like the
Also Rises"   one for "Cheers," is a one-pager. Note how well this story
                      is structured to arouse the interest of the reader, right in
                      the first paragraph:

- •   The list of stars (glamor & prestige)
- •   Ernest Hemingway's classic 1926 novel (glamor & prestige)
- •   Set in France and Spain (exotic locations)
- •   American expatriates, the lost generation, trying to find themselves (what the show is all about and what the viewer can identify with)

The second paragraph contains additional names that should be mentioned (cast, executive producer). The quote here, "one of the all-time great romantic stories," helps describe and sell the show further.

So does the third paragraph, which elaborates on what has been said. This is followed by the storyline (the next two paragraphs). The last paragraph contains the essential production information. Whenever possible, add information that will enhance the glamor and importance of what you are publicizing: "...filmed entirely on location in France and Spain...Emmy Award winner James Goldstone ("Kent State") directed..."

The longer format story runs two-and-a-half pages. It is structured differently and contains a number of additional elements. For openers, it carries a full headline, including a kicker (the information above the head) and a subhead (the names of the stars). The headline contains the essentials of the first paragraph.

The first paragraph is structured like the first paragraph of a news release. It answers the five Ws (who, what, when, where and why/how). Note how one piece of information which was contained in the last paragraph of the short storyline has been moved into the headline and the first paragraph: "... filmed entirely on location in France and Spain." This was a smart move. This information is part of the viewer appeal of this miniseries. Use this kind of information where it has the most impact -- right up front!

Note the careful wording in the way the actors are billed.

New here are the show breakdowns by days (Part I, II). This is followed by the cast list, writer and director credits. Then come the program highlights. Can you think of any other information that might have been included? How would you have written this? There's another bit of new information which we find in the first paragraph and these highlights, namely, that the miniseries is seen under the umbrella title of NBC Sunday Night at the Movies and NBC Monday Night at the Movies. It is important that you work every piece of critical information into your storylines and format stories (these umbrella titles are important to establish network identity and program continuity with viewers).

"MacGyver"   Here's another format story about a returning series. This one was prepared by an agency for a studio, in accordance with the studio's style. Studio and network styles differ. In fact, studio styles differ one from the other. If your agency is hired to prepare press kits for a network, studio, or production company, the first thing you want to do is to get two or three sample press kits from your client, so that you can study the client's style down to the last comma. You then prepare the new press kit in conformity to that style.

This format story carries a full news head. The first paragraph mentions the network broadcasting the series, the premiere month, what the series is about and who the stars and characters are. It also contains the line: "... from the Network Television Division of Paramount Pictures... ." You would not find this line in the first paragraph of a network format story. It would be in the last paragraph. So why is it in the first paragraph here? The answer is simple.

This press kit is promoting the Network TV Division of Paramount Pictures! That's your client. Always remember to put your client up front.

This format story offers details about the premiere episode and the new season. It gives information about the issues to be dramatized, the regular stars, and the guest stars.

The last paragraph lists the obligatory production information. Note how the Paramount information is repeated here, this time using the fullest legal and formal language.

The last paragraph lists the broadcast day and time. (How would you work this into the first paragraph, as some format stories do?)

"Wings"   Here's another series from Paramount, returning for another season to network television. Notice the carefully sculpted phrases:
- √ "Wings," a spirited half-hour ensemble comedy series
- √ Critically acclaimed for its rapid-fire humor, colorful characters and sophisticated edge
- √ Timothy Daly ("Almost Grown," "Diner") and Steven Weber ("The Kennedys of Massachusetts")

Notice also the well crafted descriptions of the characters. If there is something special about the production, such as the elaborate set which is used in this one, you may highlight this in your format story.

If you have never watched this series, you can get a real sense of what it's about from this format story. In addition to painting a good word picture of the series, the writer is also providing editors with good descriptive information for reviews or articles about the show.

As with "The Sun Also Rises," we are given two format stories here -- a short one and a long one. The short one is a condensed version of the long one. If you have created some good, descriptive phrases, you can use them in your various releases. Don't re-invent the wheel. Go with what you have, especially if there's no way you can improve on it.

"Degrassi High"   Here's another good example of a format story for a returning series. The first paragraph states clearly and effectively what the series is about. The second paragraph provides compelling information about the new season. We are then told more about the premiere episode (a two-parter) and some of the upcoming storylines and issues.

We are also given such other pertinent information as awards received, materials that are made available for junior and senior high school use, and special services for the hearing and visually impaired.

The final paragraph deals with the formal production credits.

"The Little This format story incorporates a number of interesting elements, **Match Girl"** made immediately apparent by the three-line double-decker headline. This format story deals with an upcoming holiday special but then uses this format story to promote three other holiday specials to be presented under the same umbrella title.

Δ **Remember that there is no such thing as an accidental or superfluous word in professional writing.** Every word counts. Every word is intended to arouse the interest of the reader and make him or her want to watch the show. Every word is meant to overcome conscious or unconscious obstacles to tuning in that show. Take a look at some of these words and phrases in the first paragraph:

√	A magical fairy tale
√	from the pen of Hans Christian Andersen
√	comes to life
√	original animated musical special
√	modern-day version of the classic story
√	exclusive presentation
√	narrated by F. Murray Abraham (1984 Best Actor Academy Award winner of "Amadeus")
√	produced and directed by Michael Sporn (HBO's "Lyle, Lyle Crocodile: The Musical" and "The Red Shoes")
√	translating favorite books into animated musical specials
√	for the entire family

The emphasis in this format story is on "The Little Match Girl," since that's the show that's being highlighted. The other three specials are mentioned in the second paragraph, with elaborations following later in the release. Remember that the format story here follows a news format. You want to make sure that your information is organized in the inverted pyramid style. If an editor decides to use only the first two paragraphs of your release, you want to make sure that those paragraphs cover all the essentials, as these do.

This information is then followed by three paragraphs of the storyline. Following the storyline are production details. Then we learn more about the other upcoming specials, including brief program information and airdates.

Study the Program Highlight at the end of the format story and compare it to the first paragraph. See how well and succinctly the storyline is stated. Note also what phrases from the first paragraph are repeated here. Log listings take skill to write. Viewers can be turned on or off by a single word!

"Kennedy Center Honors" Here's a four-page format story. Isn't that too long? The rule is: tell your story and stop. If there's a lot to tell, keep going until you have covered it all. If it's good, factual information, a longer release is justified. Of course, you must always be able to boil the essentials down to a log listing -- which you will find here, too, on the last page.

HEADS & SUBHEADS When you have a lot of information to convey in a headline, use a subhead. The head and subhead here are excellent and convey all the essential information. The first paragraph is a single sentence. So is the second paragraph. Technically speaking, they are one, since it takes the two sentences to cover the 5 Ws (who, what, when, were, and why/how). Where the sentences are this long, it looks better to break them up into two paragraphs, rather than keep them as one paragraph.

The first sentence could have been shortened, as follows:

> Five of America's most beloved and revered performers -- Dizzy Gillespie, Katharine Hepburn, Rise Stevens, Jule Styne and Billy Wilder -- are the 1990 recipients of THE KENNEDY CENTER HONORS, bestowed for achievements of excellence in the performing arts.

There's nothing wrong with this sentence. Why, then, is the actual sentence better? The classic newspaper adage states: don't underestimate people's intelligence, but don't overestimate their knowledge.

Don't assume that the reader knows what you know or "what everybody knows." Explain who these celebrities are. In doing so, you may also create additional interest in them.

Δ **Be accurate.** There is a difference between *taping* and *filming* a show. Use correct terminology, as has been done here. Note how the writer is careful in differentiating between "entertainers and celebrities" and, again, in describing the nature of their participation ("who perform or offer on-camera homage). Check your credits for the right billing information. Don't say "starring" when you should say, as here, "Making special appearances are...." Notice the last paragraph on page two. Here we talk about "filmed" capsules.

When doing format stories on events, specials or variety programs, you want to make sure to call attention to the highlights. Here you are given a full page of highlights (page 3). Note in the Highlight listing on the last page, how you can avoid billing problems when you have limited space. "Joined by" is a good phrase. (So is "appearing with.")

September 30, 1991

**RUTH SLOAN CONTACTS INFLUENTIAL FRIENDS TO TRY TO HAVE GINA
DEPORTED, AGAINST HER HUSBAND'S WISHES, ON ABC'S "HOMEFRONT"**

"Patriots" -- Ruth Sloan contacts influential friends to try to have her Italian daughter-in-law, Gina, deported. Meanwhile, Ruth's husband, Mike, realizes that Gina is his last connection to his dead son, but he doesn't know whether she will even accept his help, on "Homefront," **TUESDAY, OCT. 15** (10:00-11:00 p.m., ET), on the ABC Television Network.

Starring are Kyle Chandler as Jeff Metcalf, Sammi Davis-Voss as Caroline Hailey, Ken Jenkins as Mike Sloan, Sr., Mimi Kennedy as Ruth Sloan, Tammy Lauren as Ginger Szabo, Sterling Macer, Jr., as Robert Davis, David Newsom as Hank Metcalf, Harry O'Reilly as Charlie Hailey, Wendy Phillips as Anne Metcalf, Giuliana Santini as Gina Sloan, John Slattery as Al Kahn, Jessica Steen as Linda Metcalf, Dick Anthony Williams as Abe Davis, Alexandra Wilson as Sarah Brewer and Hattie Winston as Gloria Davis.

Guest starring are Sherry Rooney as Mrs. Mulvannety and Lee Weaver as Reverend Pastor Harrington. Co-starring are David Crowley as Agent Scott and John Di Santi as Sam.

-- -- ABC -- --

November 19, 1991

CHARLIE BECOMES THE VICTIM OF A "FATAL ATTRACTION"-TYPE PURSUIT BY A FORMER CLIENT, ON ABC'S "CIVIL WARS," DEC. 4

"Daveja Vu All Over Again" -- Charlie is the victim of a "fatal attraction-type" pursuit by a former client, Christine Sayer; Jamie Watson, the young son of an interracial marriage, is the subject of a bitter custody battle between his father, Malik, and mother, Rachel, now that Rachel has remarried; and Doris Stipes sues her husband, Sherman, for divorce after he turns their home into an arsenal in the name of security, on "Civil Wars," WEDNESDAY, DEC. 4 (10:00-11:00 p.m., ET), on the ABC Television Network.

"Civil Wars" stars Mariel Hemingway as Sydney Guilford, Peter Onorati as Charlie Howell and Debi Mazar as Denise Iannello.

"Daveja Vu All Over Again" guest stars James McDaniel as Malik Watson, Peter Jurasik as Sherman Stipes, Christine Rose as Doris Stipes, Ely Pouget as Christine Sayer, Doran Clark as Rachel Tillson, Melinda Culea as Stacy and DeVaughn W. Nixon as Jamie Watson.

-- ABC --

82

CBS Television Network
51 West 52 Street
New York 10019
November 19, 1990

MIKE'S MALPRACTICE WOES ESCALATE, ON "DOCTOR, DOCTOR," DEC. 6 ON CBS

When news about the malpractice suit becomes public, Mike's patients stop coming to see him, in Part II of a three-part episode of DOCTOR, DOCTOR, <u>Thursday, Dec. 6</u> (9:30-10:00 PM, ET/PT) on the CBS Television Network. John Neal directed from a script by Jim Herzfeld.

Mike gets into a nasty war of words on "Wake Up Providence" with the lawyer (Ann Marie Lee) who is suing him for malpractice. The result of this public feud is that Mike's patients start canceling their appointments with him, making him a liability to the practice.

Mike Stratford	Matt Frewer	Ed	Jon Menick
Abraham Butterfield	Julius J. Carry III	Hugh Persons	Brian George
Grant Linowitz	Beau Gravitte	Sheldon Boehm	Don Lake
Dierdre Bennett	Maureen Mueller	Suzanne Moore	Ann Marie Lee
Richard Stratford	Tony Carreiro	Sarah Ballantyne	Pearl Shear
Faye Barylski	Audrie J. Neenan	Mrs. Cratchit	Yvette Freeman
		Tiny Boy	Thomas Hobson

This broadcast will be captioned for deaf and hearing impaired viewers.

* * *

83

CBS Television Network
51 West 52 Street
New York 10019
November 19, 1990

**WOOD DECIDES HE HATES PLAYING HOUSEWIFE,
ON "EVENING SHADE," NOV. 26 ON CBS**

Wood has to take up the slack when Ava's job takes her further and further away from her household chores, on EVENING SHADE, <u>Monday, Nov. 26</u> (8:00-8:30 PM, ET/PT) on the CBS Television Network. David Steinberg directed from a script by Sean Daniels and David Nichols.

With her job as prosecutor taking up more time, Ava is rarely at home to cook or take care of the kids -- or Wood, who more and more has been taking up her various domestic chores and doesn't like it one bit.

Wood Newton	Burt Reynolds	Frieda Evans	Elizabeth Ashley
Ava Newton	Marilu Henner	Ponder Blue	Ossie Davis
Taylor Newton	Jay R. Ferguson	Herman Stiles	Michael Jeter
Molly Newton	Melissa Martin	Merleen Elldridge	Ann Wedgeworth
Will Newton	Jacob Parker	Nub Oliver	Charlie Dell
		Fontana Beausoleil	Linda Gehringer

This broadcast will be captioned for deaf and hearing impaired viewers.

* * *

84

BRIDESHEAD REVISITED

An eleven-part series premiering Monday, January 18, 1982
on
GREAT PERFORMANCES

"BRIDESHEAD REVISITED"

SYNOPSIS AND HIGHLIGHT LISTING

Episode Four: "Sebastian Against the World"

GREAT PERFORMANCES
Monday, February 8, 1982, 8:00-9:00 p.m. (ET)* over PBS

> "You came here as my friend; now you're
> spying on me for my mother, I know. Well
> you can get out of here and you can tell
> her from me that I'll choose my friends
> and she her spies in the future."
>
>   -- Lord Sebastian Flyte

At Brideshead Castle during the Easter vacation of 1924,
Charles Ryder (Jeremy Irons) realizes his friend Sebastian
(Anthony Andrews) is heading for trouble when he finds him drunk
in his bedroom. When Charles tries to cover up for him, Sebastian
turns on him and accuses him of being one of his mother's spies.

Later that evening, Sebastian is absent from dinner. Then,
while Lady Marchmain (Claire Bloom) reads for the rest of the
family, a hopelessly drunk Sebastian bursts into the drawing room
and interrupts the family gathering.

The next morning, Sebastian escapes from Brideshead and the
clutches of his family. Before Charles leaves, Lady Marchmain
begs Charles to try and help her son. "Sebastian is fonder of

(more....)

*(Please consult local PBS station for exact date and time.)

GREAT PERFORMANCES on PBS is a presentation of WNET/THIRTEEN, New York, and is made possible in part by a grant from EXXON
BRIDESHEAD REVISITED is produced by Granada Television International

you than any of us. You've got to help him. I can't."

But back at Oxford, Charles is incapable of preventing Sebastian's downfall. Sebastian gets drunk again and is given an ultimatum: either he must live under supervision or be expelled. Sebastian chooses to leave the university. Charles, lonely and miserable, returns home and asks his father (Sir John Gielgud) if he can leave Oxford and study art.

SUGGESTED HIGHLIGHT LISTING

GREAT PERFORMANCES, "Brideshead Revisited,"
Episode Four: Charles Ryder (Jeremy Irons)
watches helplessly as his best friend, Lord
Sebastian Flyte (Anthony Andrews), continues
on his path to self-destruction, choosing
to leave Oxford rather than submit to strict
supervision.

Made possible by a grant from EXXON and public television stations, the 11-part series, "Brideshead Revisited," is a production of Granada Television of England in association with WNET/ THIRTEEN, New York, and NDR Hamburg.

# # #

Press Contacts:

Stone Associates
Los Angeles: (213) 655-8970
New York: (212) 730-0930

WNET/THIRTEEN, New York
(212) 560-3004

Hanna-Barbera Productions, Inc.
A Subsidiary of Great American Broadcasting Company

Contact: **Media Relations**
(213) 969-1211

FANTASTIC MAX
Synopsis

Take one precocious toddler named Max, blast him into outer space, and you've got "Fantastic Max," the latest entry in Sunday Morning's "The Funtastic World of Hanna-Barbera."

"Fantastic Max" is a tyke of a different type. Max looks innocent but there's a lot going on in that little noodle.

On a trip to Cape Canaveral, Max crawled aboard a spacecraft that blasted off into deep space. He returned with a new pal: FX, from the planet Twinkle Twinkle.

FX is a pea-green little alien with magical powers. Combine magic with Max's precociousness and love for adventure, and you've got endless exciting tangles.

Trying to keep the Max and FX out of trouble is the task of A.B. Sitter, a robot made of colorful toy blocks that were obligingly zapped into life by FX.

Max's parents are oblivious to all the adventure going on around under their noses. Zoe, Max's six-year-old sister, knows Max is up to something, but can't prove it.

The sky's the limit -- literally -- as Max and FX use FX's magical powers to zap them into outer-space adventures. They can also do some pretty surprising things on earth, to the consternation of Ben, the nosy neighborhood bully.

The outer-space and earthly adventures of Max and FX promise to fill Sunday Mornings with magic for a long time to come.

THE CREDITS

Executive Producers......William Hanna
                         Joseph Barbera

Producer.................Charles A. Grosvenor

THE VOICES

Max......................Ben Ryan Ganger
FX.......................Nancy Cartwright
A. B. Sitter.............Gregg Berger
Zoe......................Elisabeth Harnois
Ben......................Benji Gregory
Mom......................Gail Matthius
Dad......................Paul Eiding

3400 Cahuenga Boulevard, Hollywood, CA 90068-Phone (213) 851-5000-FAX (213) 969-1201-Cable Address: HANBARB, Telex-67-7583

30 Rockefeller Plaza
New York, NY 10112
212 664-4444

Media Relations
National Broadcasting
Company, Inc.

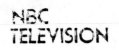

'CHEERS'

- - -

Thursdays (9–9:30 p.m. NYT) on NBC–TV

There are changes in the air as NBC–TV's Emmy Award–winning comedy series "Cheers" returns for its sixth season. The much–acclaimed program has been awarded 13 Emmys since its September 1982 premiere.

For the 1986–87 television season, "Cheers" was ranked as the third most popular television program with a 27.5 rating and a 41 share, according to the Nielsen Television Index.

In the new season, macho former Boston Red Sox star Sam Malone (Ted Danson) has sold control of his bar, Cheers, to a large corporation. Sam's new boss, the daughter of the new owner, is icy and outspoken Rebecca Howe (Kirstie Alley), with whom Malone will experience a love–hate working relationship while struggling with romantic tension.

Three–time Emmy Award winner Rhea Perlman continues in her role of feisty barmaid Carla Tortelli, who is quick with a putdown but has a heart of gold for her family.

Out–of work, beer–guzzling accountant Norm Peterson (George Wendt) and know–it–all postman Cliff Clavin (John Ratzenberger) also return, as does home-grown and dim–witted bartender Woody Boyd (Woody Harrelson).

Dr. Frasier Crane (Kelsey Grammer), too, is on hand to inject his own high–brow observations and psychological evaluations of the passing parade, of which he is now a part.

"Cheers" is a Charles/Burrows/Charles production in association with Paramount Television. James Burrows and Glen and Les Charles are the executive producers. Burrows is also the director. Peter Casey, David Lee and David Angell are the producers.

———o———

Fall, 1987

"THE SUN ALSO RISES"

Dec. 9 and 10 on NBC-TV

Jane Seymour, Hart Bochner, Robert Carradine and Leonard Nimoy star in this stylish adaptation of Ernest Hemingway's classic 1926 novel, set in France and Spain, about American expatriates and others of "the lost generation" trying to find themselves in the years following World War I.

Ian Charleson, Zeljko Ivanek, Stephane Audran and Andrea Occhipinti also star in what executive producer John Furia calls "one of the all-time great romantic stories.

"Although the setting is in the early 1920s, the human drama is very contemporary in the wake of America's involvement in Vietnam," Furia says. "Our characters all had youthful innocence until they are thrust into the dehumanizing situation of war. Now they become ghosts who live lives of excess and wild exhuberance to cover the scars of pain and tragedy."

"The Sun Also Rises" is the story of Jake Barnes (Bochner), a newspaperman who settles in Paris following World War I, and his love for the tempestuous Lady Brett Ashley (Seymour). Because of wounds suffered in the war, Jake is unable to make love and Brett destructively goes from man to man to reach some sort of unobtainable fulfillment. Her conquests include: Jake's friend, Robert Cohn (Carradine); an eccentric Russian "Count" (Nimoy); a carousing Scotsman named Mike Campbell(Charleson); and a dashing bullfighter (Occhipinti).

With Bill Gorton (Ivanek), Brett and her men go to Spain hoping to recapture something they lost in the war. That passionate journey, however, eventually leads to tragedy.

"The Sun Also Rises," filmed entirely on location in France and Spain, is a production of 20th Century Fox Television. Emmy Award-winner James Goldstone ("Kent State") directed from a teleplay by Robert L. Joseph, who is also the producer. Furia is executive producer.

——o——

November, 1984

#1114Y

89

'The Sun Also Rises' (Dec. 9 and 10)

JANE SEYMOUR AND HART BOCHNER STAR IN NBC'S 'THE SUN ALSO RISES' STYLISH FOUR-HOUR MINISERIES FILMED ENTIRELY IN FRANCE AND SPAIN

—

Leonard Nimoy, Robert Carradine, Ian Charleson,
Zeljko Ivanek and Stephane Audran also star

———————————

All the romance, grandeur and drama of Ernest Hemingway's "The Sun Also Rises" vividly comes to life in NBC-TV's four hour miniseries based on the classic novel about American expatriates living in Europe following World War I. Filmed entirely on location in Paris and Spain, "The Sun Also Rises" will be telecast on NBC Sunday Night at the Movies, Dec. 9 (9-11 p.m. NYT) and NBC Monday Night at the Movies, Dec. 10 (9-11 p.m. NYT).

Jane Seymour, Leonard Nimoy and Hart Bochner headline the international cast which also includes Robert Carradine, Ian Charleson, Zeljko Ivanek and Stephane Audran.

Emmy Award winner James Goldstone ("Kent State") directed from a teleplay by producer Robert L. Joseph. John Furia is the executive producer of the 20th Century Fox Television production.

"The Sun Also Rises" traces the turbulent lives of a group of American expatriates, members of the "Lost Generation" following World War I, who journeyed across France and Spain hoping to escape from their own memories. It focuses on American journalist Jake Barnes (Bochner), who is deeply in love with Lady Brett Ashley, a sensual English noblewoman played by Seymour. Incapacitated by a war wound, Barnes is unable to have a physical relationship with Lady Brett. Disillusioned by the war and life in general, Jake, Brett and a group of compatriots search out all the thrills and sensory pleasures Europe has to offer. Their quest leads them from the night clubs of Paris to the bullfights in Pamplona, Spain..

PART ONE

It's 1917 and Jake Barnes (Bochner), a handsome young writer, is fighting and womanizing in France during the "war to end all wars." He is wounded by a grenade that leaves him permanently scarred — both physically and emotionally.

The time shifts to 1923 and Jake, now working for the Paris-based bureau of an American newspaper, has established a new life for himself. There are friends like former pilot Bill Gorton (Ivanek), the headstrong Robert Cohn (Carradine) — and the beautiful Lady Brett Ashley (Seymour).

(more)

Because Jake and Brett's love can not be physically consumated , Brett immerses herself in the frivolities of Paris life. Cohn, Jake's fiery friend, falls in love with Brett, but she sees him as little more than another diversion. But when Brett becomes involved with another man — the unpredictable Count (Nimoy) — she is flirting with something far more dangerous than she could imagine.

PART TWO

Jake, Robert and Bill travel to Pamplona, Spain, to revitalize themselves. There they meet up with Brett and her alchoholic fiance, Mike Campbell (Charleson), for the annual running of the bulls. The Count, who is determined to get revenge for Brett's slight of him, is also there. Meanwhile, Brett sets herself up for even more problems when she begins an affair with Pedro Romero (Andrea Occhipinti), a talented young bullfighter inexperienced in the game of love.

Role	Player
Lady Brett	Jane Seymour
Jake Barnes	Hart Bochner
The Count	Leonard Nimoy
Robert Cohn	Robert Carradine
Mike Campbell	Ian Charleson
Bill Gorton	Zeljko Ivanek
Georgette	Stephane Audran
Pedro Romero	Andrea Occhipinti
Nicole	Elizabeth Bourgine
Chaz	Hutton Cobb
Frances	Jennifer Hilary
Lew Braddocks	Arch Taylor
Eve Braddocks	Renata Benedict
Gerald	Julian Firth

Writer:	Robert L. Joseph
Director:	James Goldstone

(more)

91

NBC-TV PROGRAM HIGHLIGHT DEC. 9

NBC SUNDAY NIGHT AT THE MOVIES: "The Sun Also Rises,"
Part One — Jake Barnes (Hart Bochner), a young American
journalist living in Paris following World War I, falls in love with
the beautiful and restless Lady Brett (Jane Seymour). It is a
tormented love, however, because a war wound has left Jake
physically unable to make love. Meanwhile, Brett begins to toy
with the affections of Jake's friend Robert Cohn (Robert
Carradine) and The Count, a dangerous Russian emigre (Leonard
Nimoy).

NBC-TV PROGRAM HIGHLIGHT DEC. 10

NBC MONDAY NIGHT AT THE MOVIES: "The Sun Also Rises,"
Part Two — Jake (Hart Bochner), Robert (Robert Carradine) and
Bill (Zeljko Ivanek) travel to Pamplona, Spain, for the annual
running of the bulls and meet up with Lady Brett (Jane Seymour)
and her fiance, Mike Campbell (Ian Charleson). Jealousy over
Brett results in tragedy. Leonard Nimoy also stars.

PRESS REP.: Barry Cherin, Movies and Miniseries Publicity, 818/840-3651

—o—

November, 1984
#1185Y

"MacGYVER" RETURNS FOR SIXTH SEASON

AFTER STRONG SPRING FINISH

After a strong finish in the ratings last spring, "MacGYVER," the hour-long action/adventure series from the Network Television Division of Paramount Pictures, returns to ABC in September 1990 for its sixth season. Richard Dean Anderson stars as MacGyver, the non-violent, quick-witted hero who uses his ingenuity and scientific knowledge to solve problems and complete dangerous missions. Dana Elcar returns as MacGyver's boss and friend, Pete Thornton, director of field operations for The Phoenix Foundation.

In the season premiere episode, titled "Humanity," MacGyver and Pete Thornton travel to Romania as part of an international delegation sent to assess the unearthed archives of deposed Romanian dictator Nikolai Ceausescu. Later episodes will focus on the "life" of a gun, teenage alcoholism, the farm labor movement and the use of pesticides, and the aftermath of the fall of the Berlin wall. The series will also continue to address environmental concerns -- such as the plight of dolphins and bears, and the depletion of the aquifer -- as it has since it premiered in 1985. A sequel to last season's popular fantasy/western episode ("Serenity") is also planned, as well as a season-finale centering on the three Colton brothers (played by Richard Lawson, Cleavon Little and Cuba Gooding, Jr., who have all been recurring guest-stars on "MacGYVER" for the last two seasons).

A HENRY WINKLER/JOHN RICH PRODUCTION
in association with

93

Mayim Bialik (now starring in her own series) will return in her recurring role as Lisa, as will W. Morgan Sheppard as Dr. Zito and Kim Zimmer (who just won her third Emmy for "The Guiding Light") as Murphy. In addition, a new love interest for MacGyver will be introduced early in the season.

"MacGYVER" is a Henry Winkler/John Rich Production in association with the Network Television Division of Paramount Pictures, a Paramount Communications company. Henry Winkler, John Rich and Steve Downing are executive producers. Michael Greenburg is supervising producer and John Moranville is co-producer.

"MacGYVER" airs Mondays at 8:00 p.m. (ET) on ABC-TV.

\#   \#   \#

CONTACT: Rebeca Manning (213/659-9111)
            Judy Katz (212/247-2320)
            RICHARD GRANT & ASSOCIATES

            John Wentworth (213/956-5394)
            VP, Ad/Pub/Promo
            Network Television Division
            PARAMOUNT PICTURES

082890

ABOUT 'WINGS'

"Wings," a spirited half-hour ensemble comedy series from Grub Street Productions in association with the Network Television Division of Paramount Pictures, returns to NBC this fall on Friday nights at 9:30 PM. Critically acclaimed for its rapid-fire humor, colorful characters and sophisticated edge, the half-hour comedy features a strong ensemble cast backed by one of the most creative and successful writing and producing teams in television.

Created and executive produced by Emmy Award winners David Angell, Peter Casey and David Lee, former supervising producers/writers of "Cheers," "Wings" stars Timothy Daly ("Almost Grown," "Diner") and Steven Weber ("The Kennedys of Massachusetts") as Joe and Brian Hackett, brothers who operate Sandpiper Air, a small commuter airline on the island of Nantucket. Joe, the proud owner, is a compulsively well-organized model of responsibility and is often exasperated by his free-wheeling, mischievous younger brother, Brian, a good-natured rogue. Though perfect opposites in style and temperament, both

(more...)

Grub Street Productions
in association with

95

5555 Melrose Avenue, Hollywood, CA 90038-3197 (213) 956-5000

are pilots who share a passion for flying.

The Hacketts are surrounded by a lively and opinionated group of airport regulars, including series star Crystal Bernard ("It's A Living," "Happy Days") as Helen Chappel, an attractive young woman who runs the airport lunch counter and moonlights as a cello teacher; David Schramm as Roy Biggins, the brash and overbearing owner of Joe's rival airline, Aeromass; Rebecca Schull as Fay Evelyn Cochran, a relentlessly cheerful ex-stewardess in her 60's who runs the Sandpiper Air ticket counter; and Thomas Haden Church as Lowell Mather, the laconic, blue-collar airport maintenance man.

Much of the comedy in "Wings" emanates from the "odd couple" relationship between the Hackett brothers. The controlled, buttoned-down Joe finds it impossible to fathom how his irresponsible brother could have blown his opportunities for a Princeton education and NASA astronaut training; the high-spirited, irresistably charming and quick-witted Brian finds it equally difficult to deal with his brother's overly compulsive behavior.

Adding to the comedic tension is the brothers' relationship with Helen. The three, having once enjoyed an easy childhood friendship, now find it necessary to redefine their relationship as adults, a situation which prompts many awkward and funny moments.

Set in a small regional airport on Nantucket Island, "Wings" allows the cast to interact with an endless stream of visitors, from gypsies to jet-setters. The unavoidable interplay between

(more...)

the locals and the tourists provides additional opportunities for comic situations.

The elaborate "Wings" set, designed by four-time Emmy Award-winning art director Roy Christopher, houses a hangar containing the body of an actual nine-seat Cessna 402 airplane and an ingeniously designed two-level terminal area which includes Helen's lunch counter. These exciting visual elements, combined with outstanding writing and the impressive on-camera chemistry among the actors, have made "Wings" one of the brightest new comedies on television.

Joining series Creators/Executive Producers David Angell, Peter Casey and David Lee for the production are Roz Doyle ("The Slap Maxwell Story," "The Days and Nights of Molly Dodd") as producer, Dave Hackel ("Dear John") as supervising producer, and Philip LaZebnik ("Day By Day") and Bruce Rasmussen ("Anything But Love") as co-producers. Noam Pitlik will direct all episodes this season.

"Wings" is a Grub Street Production in association with the Network Television Division of Paramount Pictures. Paramount Pictures is a Paramount Communications company.

\# \# \#

CONTACT:
Leah Krantzler 213/965-1990
Marisa Spitz 212/986-7080
THE LIPPIN GROUP

John A. Wentworth 213/956-5394
V.P., Ad./Pub./Promo.
Network Television Division
PARAMOUNT PICTURES

A Grub Street Production in association with
Paramount Network Television
for NBC-TV

STARRING...................................Timothy Daly
                                           Steven Weber
                                           Crystal Bernard
                                           Thomas Haden Church
                                           David Schramm
                                           Rebecca Schull

CREATORS/EXECUTIVE PRODUCERS................David Angell
                                           Peter Casey
                                           David Lee

SUPERVISING PRODUCER.......................Dave Hackel

PRODUCER...................................Roz Doyle

CO-PRODUCERS...............................Philip LaZebnik
                                           Bruce Rasmussen

ASSOCIATE PRODUCER.........................Maggie Randell

"Wings," Paramount Network Television's spirited half-hour
ensemble comedy, stars Timothy Daly and Steven Weber as Joe and
Brian Hackett, brothers who operate Sandpiper Air, a fledgling
commuter airline on the island of Nantucket. Joe, the proud
owner, is a compulsively well-organized model of responsibility,
and is often exasperated by his free-wheeling and mischievous
younger brother Brian. Though perfect opposites in temperament,
both are pilots and share a passion for flying.

The Hacketts are surrounded by a lively and opinionated
group of airport regulars, including series stars Crystal Bernard

(more...)

Grub Street Productions
in association with

Paramount
A Paramount Communications Company

98
5555 Melrose Avenue, Hollywood, CA 90038-3197 (213) 956-5000

as Helen Chappel, an attractive young woman who runs the airport
lunch counter and moonlights as a cello teacher; David Schramm as
Roy Biggins, the brash and overbearing owner of Joe's rival
airline, Aeromass; Rebecca Schull as Fay Evelyn Cochran, a
relentlessly cheerful ex-stewardess in her 60's who runs the
Sandpiper Air ticket counter; and Thomas Haden Church as Lowell
Mather, the laconic blue-collar airport maintenance man.

The "odd couple" interplay between the two brothers,
compounded by their relationship with Helen, form the basis of
this sophisticated character comedy which unfolds each week in a
small-town airport setting.

CONTACTS: Leah Krantzler   213/965-1990
                   Marisa Spitz   212/986-7080
                   THE LIPPIN GROUP

                   John A. Wentworth   213/956-5394
                   V.P., Ad./Pub./Promo.
                   Network Television Division
                   PARAMOUNT PICTURES

"DEGRASSI HIGH" RETURNS FOR LAST SEMESTER

Joey, Wheels, Snake, Lucy, Caitlin, and the rest of the Degrassi gang are back in new episodes, dealing with the ups and downs of teenage life, not realizing this will be their last semester at Degrassi High.

This season, the 13-part series covers the serious topics of AIDS, sexual abuse, academic difficulties, drugs, and suicide. As always, the storylines are tempered with lighter plots and subplots involving first kisses, talent shows, dating, slumber and poker parties, friendship, and the prom. The new season begins Saturday, April 6, 1991, 7:30 - 8:00 p.m. ET* and continues through June 29, 1991.

In the two-part premiere episode, "Bad Blood," Joey continues to be badgered by his nemesis, Dwayne, who tries to sabotage his chances of winning enough money to buy a car. In a more serious vein, one of the students tests HIV positive and must face the spectre of AIDS. Safe sex becomes an issue when condom machines are installed in the bathrooms.

Later in the season, Liz starts to date Patrick, which forces her to confront painful childhood memories of sexual abuse. Wheels, still trying to cope with the death of his parents, is neglecting his school and home responsibilities. Tired of his lies and excuses, his grandmother finally asks him to move out. Caitlin reacts with disbelief and anger when she discovers her father is having an affair. And the entire school is shocked and saddened when a student commits suicide.

-more-

*Check local listings

On the lighter side, Lucy continues videotaping Degrassi chronicles for her friend L.D., who is recovering from leukemia. While she tapes student reaction to the new condom machines in the school restrooms, Dwayne discovers they make great water bombs to drop on unsuspecting classmates.

All night parties offer poker games—and marijuana. Tessa and Yankou discover the joys of budding romance, aided by matchmaker Arthur. And breakups and reconciliations abound as Michelle, B.L.T., Cindy, Snake, Liz, Patrick, Spike, Simon, Alexa, Bronco, Lucy, Joey, and Caitlin form new alliances and strengthen old friendships.

In the series' conclusion, essential renovations at Degrassi High close the school—ending four successful seasons of the popular series.

DEGRASSI HIGH continues to win awards and recognition by educators as an effective teaching tool in the classroom. Some of the most recent awards include the National Educational Association award and the Nancy Susan Reynolds Award for outstanding portrayal of family planning and sexuality issues in the media from the Center for Population Options.

DEGRASSI HIGH is accompanied by a discussion and activity guide ($3.00); student newspaper ($1.00 or $10.00 per classroom set of 25) for junior high and senior high school use. To order materials for the new season, write WGBH, DEGRASSI Term 5, Box 2222-DH, South Easton, MA 02375.

The series is closed captioned for the hearing impaired and is distributed in descriptive video for the visually impaired.

DEGRASSI HIGH is produced by Playing With Time, Inc. and WGBH Boston with Taylor Productions, Inc., in association with the Canadian Broadcasting Corporation (CBC). The series is funded by the Corporation for Public Broadcasting, public television stations, the Carnegie Corporation of New York, the John D. and Catherine T. MacArthur Foundation, the Canadian Broadcasting Corporation, and Telefilm, Canada. Executive producers: Kate Taylor and Linda Schuyler. Producer/director: Kit Hood.

# # #

Winter/Spring 1991

101

Home Box Office
Media Relations

1100 Avenue of the Americas
New York, NY 10036
(212) 512-1000

**FAMILY
PROGRAMMING**

For Immediate Release

Nov. 16, 1990

THE LITTLE MATCH GIRL COMES TO LIFE IN THE HBO STORYBOOK MUSICALS
ADAPTATION OF HANS CHRISTIAN ANDERSEN'S CLASSIC FAIRY TALE,
DEBUTING DEC. 6, EXCLUSIVELY ON HBO

————

Special Presentations Of **Babar And Father Christmas**,
The Trolls And The Christmas Express And **The Magic Circus: Cirque Du Soleil**
Also Highlight The Holiday Season On HBO

————

A magical fairy tale from the pen of Hans Christian Andersen comes to life on the HBO service in

December when the original animated musical special HBO STORYBOOK MUSICALS: THE LITTLE MATCH

GIRL is presented MONDAY, DEC. 10 (7:00-7:30 p.m. ET). A modern-day version of the classic story, this

exclusive presentation is narrated by F. Murray Abraham (1984 Best Actor Academy Award® winner for

"Amadeus"), and produced and directed by Michael Sporn (HBO's "Lyle, Lyle Crocodile: The Musical" and

"The Red Shoes"). THE LITTLE MATCH GIRL is the latest in the HBO STORYBOOK MUSICALS series

translating favorite books into animated musical specials for the entire family.

(Please note additional playdates include: Dec. 6, 19 and 24.)

HBO STORYBOOK MUSICALS: THE LITTLE MATCH GIRL highlights the holiday season on HBO,

also featuring special presentations of the animated family favorites "Babar and Father Christmas," "The Trolls

and the Christmas Express" and the colorful Emmy-winning special "The Magic Circus: Cirque du Soleil."

It's New Year's Eve 1999, and as most New Yorkers prepare to celebrate, a homeless family takes

refuge in an abandoned subway station. Their little girl, Angela, ventures into the cold evening and

befriends a stray dog named Albert while on her way to sell matches to theater-goers in Times Square. Blue

(more)

® Academy Award and Oscar are registered trademarks and service marks of the Academy of Motion Picture Arts and
Sciences.

102

Contact: New York: Nancy Lesser or Tim Chandler (212) 512-1607 or 1462
              Los Angeles: Richard Licata or Mara Mikialian (213) 201-9274 or 9276

and lonely, and having no success selling matches, Angela and Albert hide from the freezing wind in a vacant lot. When Angela strikes a match for warmth, the ghost of her favorite aunt appears and whisks them off to the Botanical Gardens, where wealthy people attend a gala benefit for the homeless. They all dance to the orchestra's music, but when the reverie ends, Angela and Albert are back in the vacant lot.

Lighting another match, Angela sees her favorite street musician blowing on his sax. He takes Angela and Albert to Central Park, where the little girl and her dog enjoy a jam session under a huge tent. When the music's over and Angela is back in the cold night, she strikes a third match. Her grandmother appears and takes them downtown, where a luxury apartment tower has risen on the site of Angela's former home, a tenement building. The wind picks up and the snow starts falling harder, but nobody comes to the aid of the little girl and her dog.

Early the next morning, a crowd gathers around the frozen figure of Angela in a corner of Union Square. Each person recognizes her, but they don't seem to know what to do. It takes the healing arms of her mother to revive Angela -- and awaken the conscience of New Yorkers on New Year's Day.

Continuing the tradition of such acclaimed HBO presentations as "Lyle, Lyle Crocodile: The Musical" and the Emmy-nominated "Madeline," HBO STORYBOOK MUSICALS translate favorite books into animated musical specials for the entire family. Upcoming presentations include Beatrix Potter's "Peter Rabbit," with the voice of Carol Burnett and music by Sheldon Harnick ("Fiddler on the Roof") and Stephen Lawrence, debuting next Easter.

THE LITTLE MATCH GIRL is a production of Michael Sporn Animation, Inc.; produced and directed by Michael Sporn; written by Maxine Fisher, adapted from the tale by Hans Christian Andersen; executive producer, Giuliana Nicodemi; music by Caleb Sampson; narrator, F. Murray Abraham.

Also highlighting the holiday season on HBO, the popular storybook elephant Babar comes to life in BABAR AND FATHER CHRISTMAS. This animated presentation follows King Babar as he visits Santa Claus and invites him to visit the children in the tropical land of Celesteville. Laurent de Brunhoff narrates. Playdates include Dec. 13, 21 and 24.

In the animated family film THE TROLLS AND THE CHRISTMAS EXPRESS, six trouble-making trolls try to sabotage Santa Claus -- but he puts Christmas back on track by engineering a plan to deliver his

103

(more)

presents by train. Playdates include Dec. 20 and 25.

THE MAGIC CIRCUS: CIRQUE DU SOLEIL features seven mesmerizing acts, including daring aerialists and high-wire performers, a serpentine contortionist, acrobats, cyclists and a jovial master clown, in this HBO special featuring the critically acclaimed Canadian circus troupe. Taped in Montreal, the special features Cirque du Soleil's exquisite lighting and special effects, fanciful costumes, delightful choreography and enchanting musical score. The show received an Emmy Award in 1989 in the category of Outstanding Special Events. Playdates include Dec. 14, 20, 22 and 25.

PROGRAM HIGHLIGHT -- MONDAY, DEC. 10 (7:00-7:30 p.m. ET)

HBO STORYBOOK MUSICALS: THE LITTLE MATCH GIRL -- Set in New York City, this adaptation of Hans Christian Andersen's enduring fairy tale tells how a plucky homeless girl copes with a bitterly cold New Year's Eve 1999, and how the city's residents are taught a valuable lesson in compassion. Narrated by F. Murray Abraham ("Amadeus"), the exclusive HBO animated family special is produced and directed by Michael Sporn ("Lyle, Lyle Crocodile: The Musical").

Mark of Excellence
Presentations

Press Representative:
Owen Comora Associates
425 Madison Avenue
NY, NY 10017
Tel: 212/750-5556
Fax: 212/750-0183

"KENNEDY CENTER HONORS," STAR-STUDDED SALUTE TO FIVE LEGENDS,

SET AS 'GM MARK OF EXCELLENCE PRESENTATION' DEC. 28 ON CBS

Gillespie, Hepburn, Stevens, Styne and Wilder Honored

In 13th National Celebration of Performing Arts

———

Five of America's most beloved and revered performers--jazz
trumpeter Dizzy Gillespie, legendary actress Katharine Hepburn,
mezzo-soprano Rise Stevens, composer Jule Styne and film
director/writer Billy Wilder--are the 1990 recipients of THE
KENNEDY CENTER HONORS, bestowed for achievements of excellence in
the performing arts.

The event, the 13th annual national celebration of the
performing arts, was taped at The Kennedy Center Opera House and
will be the subject of a special two-hour GM MARK OF EXCELLENCE
PRESENTATION, Friday, December 28 (9-11 p.m. ET) on CBS-TV.

First Lady Barbara Bush and Vice President and Mrs. Dan
Quayle join a galaxy of stars, political dignitaries, celebrities
and other notables in the audience in a packed Kennedy Center
Opera House where tribute is paid to Gillespie, the standard-
setting jazzman; Hepburn, whose very name has become synonymous
with American film; Stevens, who elevated opera to its highest
level; Styne, a leading composer in American musical theater; and

(more)

105

Wilder, the celebrated director/writer producer of innumerable cinema masterpieces.

Host Walter Cronkite, described once as "the most trusted man in America," is joined on the telecast by a star-spangled array of entertainers and celebrities who perform or offer on-camera homage to the Honorees, each of whom has made an individual mark of excellence in the performing arts.

Making special appearances are: Lauren Bacall, Glenn Close, Bill Cosby, Tyne Daly, Marilyn Horne, Jack Jones, Angela Lansbury, Jack Lemmon, Hal Linden, Walter Matthau, Maureen McGovern, Aprile Millo, Ann Reinking, Jerome Robbins and Tommy Tune.

Footage of a White House reception for the Honorees, hosted by President and Mrs. George Bush, is included in the telecast, as well as special filmed capsule biographies on each Honoree, a tradition begun with the first telecast of THE KENNEDY CENTER HONORS. This year's capsule biographies, which include filmed excerpts from the Honorees' past performances, were produced under the supervision of the program's executive producers, George Stevens Jr. and Nick Vanoff. The biographies were written, researched and produced by Cathy Shields and Sara Lukenson.

Among the program highlights:

(more)

--Bill Cosby offers a tribute to Gillespie; and the jazzman's band, the United Nation Orchestra, cooks with a rendition of "A Night In Tunisia."

--Marilyn Horne lauds her fellow mezzo-soprano, Stevens, and soprano Aprile Millo performs a thrilling rendition of "La Mama Morta," from the opera "Andrea Chenier." Julius Rudel conducts.

--Actresses Glenn Close and Lauren Bacall join Angela Lansbury in reading passages by and about the legendary Katharine Hepburn, who becomes the recipient of an emotionally-charged two standing ovations from the audience in the jammed Kennedy Center Opera House.

--Buchwald, who might very well be described as America's "satirist laureate," serves up a humorous look at the role of the press in international diplomacy.

--Jack Lemmon and Walter Matthau toast Billy Wilder and reminisce about what it was like to work with one of America's premiere directors. James Naughton, Gregg Edelman and Shawn Elliot perform a scene from "City of Angels," this year's Tony winner as Best Broadway Musical.

--Jerome Robbins, 1981 Kennedy Center Honoree, praises Styne in a segment which includes Tyne Daly, Jack Jones, Hal Linden and Maureen McGovern in a medley of Styne's hits, including: "Everything's Coming Up Roses"; "It Seems I've Heard That Song Before"; "It's Magic"; "People"; "The Party's Over"; and "Some

(more)

People." Tommy Tune and Ann Reinking sing and dance to "Just In

Time."

The GM MARK OF EXCELLENCE PRESENTATIONS represent General

Motors' major, multi-million dollar commitment to excellence,

manifested in the company's sponsorship of multiple, high-quality

series and specials on the commercial networks (ABC,CBS and NBC),

public television (PBS), and cable (A&E Cable Network).

"THE KENNEDY CENTER HONORS":
"GM MARK OF EXCELLENCE PRESENTATION" HIGHLIGHT
FOR FRIDAY, DEC. 28 ON CBS

THE KENNEDY CENTER HONORS-Five legendary performing artists--
Dizzy Gillespie, Katharine Hepburn, Rise Stevens, Jule Styne and
Billy Wilder--are the recipients of the 1990 Kennedy Center
Honors, for achievements of excellence in the performing arts.
Host Walter Cronkite is joined in the tributes by Bill Cosby,
Lauren Bacall, Angela Lansbury, Jack Lemmon, Walter Matthau,
Glenn Close, Hal Linden, Marilyn Horne, Tyne Daly, Maureen
McGovern, Tommy Tune, Ann Reinking, Jack Jones, Art Buchwald and
others.
                         # # # #
December, 1990

6

ITEMS & PRODUCTION NOTES

Items are mini-news stories or mini-feature stories. They are anywhere from four lines to 24 lines in length, give or take a few lines. Production notes are the same thing.

Items differ from production notes in that each item repeats the basic program information (name of the show, date, time, and station). Production notes are written as a single document, with one piece of information following the other, paragraph after paragraph. Items, on the other hand, are set apart from each other, each often carrying its own headline or "slug line" (a catchy word or phrase above the item or on the same line as the first sentence, serving the same function as a headline).

Generally speaking, television press kits tend to contain this kind of information in the form of items, while motion picture press kits use the production notes format (please see Chapter 10).

Whatever they're called, items or production notes serve several valuable functions.

- They can be planted with columnists in the course of your publicity campaign. You can plant several items with the same columnist that way, one at a time at appropriate intervals, thus keeping interest alive in your show.

- Columnists usually want their items on an exclusive basis. After the columnist has used the item, you can recycle it and use it in your press kit for general distribution.

- Every press kit should contain one or more pages of column items or production notes. They stimulate interest and may lead to interviews and other forms of coverage.

- Items can serve as the springboard to fuller stories which you can pursue with the media. As you gather information, think of what else you can do with it, besides releasing it as an item. Is there a visual story here for the print media? What about the broadcast media? Is this the kind of thing that Entertainment Tonight, for instance, might want to cover? Is this something that you might want to shoot and make available to the print or broadcast media? If so, you may want your still photographer or film crew (hired to get B-roll and other footage for your electronic press kit) provide coverage.

Δ **There are two kinds of items:** news items and human interest items. News items are self-evident: announcement story, start of production story, casting information, for example. Even though these are often written as a longer news release, from one to two pages in length, the release frequently ends up as a one-paragraph item in a newspaper or trade publication.

Δ **News items.** Not all items appear in someone's column. Sometimes an item stands alone as a one-paragraph news story, often referred to as a news item. That's another meaning of the word "item," i.e., a brief reference.

Δ **Other names.** Items are also known as briefs, fillers, shorts, and notes, and they are sometimes listed in newspaper sections and trade publications under such special headings.

Δ **Human interest item.** The other kind of item is the human interest item. A human interest item deals with anything that is unusual, unexpected, provocative, humorous, intriguing, or otherwise fascinating. You find these items by keeping your eyes and ears open while covering a show. You may see something in a star's bio and suddenly make a connection between that and his current show. Special effects, wardrobe, and makeup are often great sources for items. Unusual props, sets and locations can become item subjects. The items that have been included here are for the most part all human interest items.

"The Sun Also Rises" items are worth studying. They are good examples of really short items. Notice how well written they are. The writer has used an economy of words. These items are polished little gems. Notice how they are set up to get and hold your interest, from the head (headline) to the first sentence, all the way to the last sentence.

These items would have been about a line longer had they included the broadcast date and time.

The **"Sarah, Plain and Tall"** items run anywhere from 11 to 19 lines. Note the various subject matter:
- The producing debut of Glenn Close and how she came upon this story
- The executive producer's thoughts on what made the book on which this show is based a classic
- What made the author entrust her work to Glenn Close
- Glenn Close's thoughts on producing
- What made the author write this story in the first place
- The acting debut of six-year-old Christopher Bell and what made him go into acting
- How the book became an unexpected hit
- The story behind the farm where the show was filmed

- The story behind the steam engine
- The author's reaction to Glenn Close's handling of her book

As you read these items, think of what else you could do with the material besides planting an item with a columnist. Which two items in particular have a visual story connected with them? Are these print stories or TV entertainment news stories or both? If you had a film crew working for you, what footage might be useful to you? What would you do with it?

These items, too, are well written. Notice how the following key information is repeated each time: **...a HALLMARK HALL OF FAME presentation of "Sarah, Plain and Tall," starring Glenn Close and Christopher Walken, airs on CBS Sunday, February 3, 1991.** The reason you want to repeat this information with each item is to make sure that your most important message -- your plug, your commercial -- does not get left to chance or lost in the shuffle. An editor, under pressure of deadline, might not take the time to look for it and add it, or he may leave out some part of it that's important to you (the network's name or the sponsor's name). There's no guarantee, of course, that your item, or your commercial message, will get used in full, but you improve your chances if you provide full information.

The nine **GM MARK OF EXCELLENCE PRESENTATION** items are all, well, excellent. The Katharine Hepburn item was unscripted and happened when the show was being taped. Because of its spontaneous, unprecedented, and topical nature, and because of Hepburn's major star status, the item should be easy to plant and create additional, last-minute interest in the special.

What do you notice that's different about these items? That's right, they're single spaced, not double-spaced. Items are often single-spaced, because you can get more on a page that way. Is one way right and the other way wrong? Not really. I've written them both ways. Double-spaced copy tends to be easier to read and edit, which is why press materials are usually double-spaced (and printed on one side of the page). However, I have seen copy from major companies where the biographies are single-spaced and news releases are printed on both sides of the page. In some cases this is done out of budgetary considerations, in other cases out of environmental considerations. The majority of press releases, however, are still printed on one side of the page, double spaced.

Δ **Sponsors.** Now for a word *about* the sponsor...Hallmark...General Motors, and others. Some major sponsors have worked their names into the generic, umbrella title of their programs: a HALLMARK HALL OF FAME Presentation ...a GM MARK OF EXCELLENCE PRESENTATION. Some television newspapers and magazines have a policy against using the sponsor's name so cleverly worked into the title. They simply drop the product name and shorten the title. HALLMARK HALL OF FAME becomes HALL OF FAME and GM MARK OF EXCELLENCE PRESENTATION becomes MARK OF EXCELLENCE PRESENTATION. This is a publication's editorial prerogative. You, the publicist, have no editorial control over this. However, you must always list the full name in your copy. That way you are off the hook. If the sponsor wants to make sure that his name is associated with the show, he needs to take out an ad (which is the reason some papers have this editorial policy in the first place).

Finally, on the subject of sponsors, take a a look at the second item on the second page. It's all about General Motors -- and it's a perfectly legitimate item. It points out that GM is sponsoring THE KENNEDY CENTER HONORS for the eighth consecutive year and mentions other GM MARK OF EXCELLENCE PRESENTATIONS that are coming up (and which have been announced previously). This item may not get picked up by itself, but it is a nice compact statement of GM's TV involvement and may get dropped into an article about this particular special. Even if it does not get used, the fact that it's in the press kit will make the sponsor happy.

'THE SUN ALSO RISES'
Column Items

ROLE REVERSAL

In NBC-TV's "The Sun Also Rises," Hart Bochner plays a young American journalist in love with the sensual Lady Brett Ashley (played by Jayne Seymour). That's quite a switch from their relationship in another miniseries, "East of Eden." In that one, Seymour was Bochner's mother.

*

GUEST APPEARANCE

Margaux Hemingway, neice of Ernest Hemingway, paid a surprise visit to the set of NBC-TV's "The Sun Also Rises" during filming at the Bal Musette nightclub in Paris. Hemingway, who was taping a documentary on her famous uncle, went so far as to leave her signature on the wall. Sharp-eyed viewers of the miniseries might just be able to spot her distinctive autograph.

*

THE 'COCO' LOOK

Jane Seymour's dark wig with bob for NBC-TV's "The Sun Also Rises" caused her daughter to refer to her as 'Prince Charming.' Actually, the specially created (circa 1920) wig is meant to emulate the look of Coco Chanel, the legendary Paris fashion designer.

*

NO BULL

Executive producer John Furia believes in taking great risks to get what he wants on film. For NBC-TV's "The Sun Also Rises," he rode in a small camera truck that was being chased by angry bulls for a special action sequence. The bulls were fast and gained on the camera truck — which pulled into a fenced pen just feet behind the rampaging bulls. Furia was not about to do a second "take."

*

PARIS ON PARADE

NBC's "The Sun Also Rises" will provide viewers with an opulent tour of Paris. Director James Goldstone managed to utilize such well-known locations as Versailles, Place de Voges, Eiffel Tower, Place Dauphine, Place de la Concorde, Pont Neuf and Pont Alexandre III. Goldstone"s biggest problem was camouflaging television aerials for the Paris of 1920 he was trying to capture.

113

(more)

LOST GENERATION

Jane Seymour likens the characters in NBC-TV's "The Sun Also Rises" to today's punk rockers. "They too were a generation that lived on the edge. Their lives were like a bullfight, a constant flirtation with death and danger."

*

TURNING POINT

Robert L. Joseph, a Hemingway afficienado who adapted "The Sun Also Rises" into a 4-hour NBC miniseries, says this about the book's initial reception: "Hemingway hadn't been too successful prior to the publication of 'The Sun Also Rises' but this book did it for him. The reviews were great. However, F. Scott Fitzgerald talked him into dropping the first two chapters prior to publication; Hemingway's mother didn't like the book; and a friend who clearly saw himself as the inspiration for one of the characters, threatened to kill Hemingway."

*

FANCY DRESS

The dress that Jane Seymour wears as she does a mad Charleston on a cafe table in NBC-TV's "The Sun Also Rises" is no mere costume. It is a Chanel original designed by the great Coco Chanel herself in the mid-1920's. The dress was borrowed from the House of Chanel Museum in Paris and is priceless.

*

COMPLEX LADY

Jane Seymour sums up her Lady Brett Ashley character in NBC-TV's "The Sun Also Rises" as follows: "Lady Brett is always drunk, but never shows it. She's several different personalities in one woman. She can't have the man she really loves so she compensates by falling in love with most of the other men who come into her life."

*

(more)

HOT TIME

John Furia, executive producer of NBC-TV's "The Sun Also Rises," hired 500 extras to work in a fiesta sequence in Segovia, Spain. He feared he'd have an unhappy crowd on his hands when the sun got hotter and hotter during the filming. But when the scene ended and the extras were dismissed, they refused to leave. They were having too much fun.

*

FANCY CLOTHES

"The Sun Also Rises" promises to offer viewers a parade of fashions. All ten of Jane Seymour's costumes are from the House of Chanel and five of them are from Chanel's 1984 summer line. The men's clothes were designed by Cerruti 1881.

*

SOBERING ROLE

What's the greatest challenge for Ian Charleson ("Chariots of Fire") in playing the carousing Mike Campbell in NBC-TV's "The Sun Also Rises?" "The most difficult thing about the role," says Charleson "is be play drunk all the time without appearing ridiculous."

*

—o—

November, 1984
#1221Y

115

Sarah
PLAIN AND TALL

COLUMN ITEMS

GLENN CLOSE ON 'SARAH' -- "Sarah, Plain and Tall," the HALLMARK HALL OF FAME presentation airing on CBS <u>Sunday, February 3, 1991</u>, marks the producing debut of Glenn Close, one of the world's most accomplished and popular actresses.   Close became familiar with "Sarah" when she recorded Patricia MacLachlan's Newbery Medal-winning children's story for Caedmon Tapes. "There's a good reason it's regarded as a classic, even though it was published just five years ago," says Close. "The story of Sarah bringing love to a lonely, motherless family touches a deep chord within us all. The story is told from a child's perspective, but it's really very adult, because there's a great love story going on, which the child isn't aware of.

"It's a very delicate tale, and the writing is just wondrous. I'm amazed at how many people have come up to me and said, 'I hear you're doing "Sarah" -- it's one of the finest books I've ever read.' I believe this story is going to become part of our national sensibility."

# # #

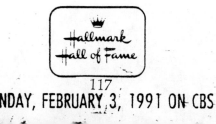

SUNDAY, FEBRUARY 3, 1991 ON CBS

NICE STEPMOTHER -- According to William Self, executive producer (along with Glenn Close) of the HALLMARK HALL OF FAME presentation of "Sarah, Plain and Tall," airing on CBS <u>Sunday, February 3, 1991</u>, there are several reasons why the book upon which it is based has become a classic in just five years. "It's about love," says Self, "it's about family, it's about relationships, and it's about a nice stepmother." In the Newbery Medal-winning book (by Patricia MacLachlan), Sarah (played by Glenn Close) leaves the safety and security of her Maine roots and journeys to Kansas, in response to a newspaper ad placed by lonely widower Jacob Witting (Christopher Walken), who has two young children. "Stepmothers have been picked on forever," says Self. "They're like mothers-in-law. But this is a nice stepmother story. It shows that a stranger can come into a family and love the children as if they were her own. There are a lot of adopted children in America, and a lot of stepmothers, and we think 'Sarah' is going to have special meaning for them."

# # #

PLACING TRUST -- Following publication of <u>Sarah, Plain and Tall</u>, the Newbery Medal-winning tale of life in Kansas in the early 1900s, author Patricia MacLachlan received offers from several film companies that wanted to buy the rights to her celebrated book, one million copies of which are now in print. She turned all the would-be suitors down. "I was in no hurry to part with the rights," MacLachlan remembers. "Somehow I knew that the right person with the right sensibilities would come along, and a film would get made that would do justice to the characters and the story." That person turned out to be Glenn Close. Close contacted the author after recording <u>Sarah</u> for Books on Tape. "I could tell about two minutes into the conversation that this woman and I were on the same wavelength," MacLachlan remembers. "I knew she'd treat my work with respect and love, and having seen the completed film, I know placing my trust in her was one of the smartest decisions of my professional life." Close is executive producer (along with William Self) of the HALLMARK HALL OF FAME presentation, which airs on CBS <u>Sunday, February 3, 1991</u>; she also stars in the title role. MacLachlan wrote the script, with Carol Sobieski. Did the author/scriptwriter ever tire of "Sarah" which, after all, took six years from first book manuscript to finished film? "Absolutely not," she says. "I got to know the characters better over the years. The original book was very spare, and adding characters and plot just came naturally. The whole experience has been a labor of love."

# # #

PRODUCER SECRET — What's the secret of being a successful television producer? Glenn Close, executive producer (along with William Self) of the HALLMARK HALL OF FAME presentation of "Sarah, Plain and Tall," airing on CBS <u>Sunday, February 3, 1991</u>, thinks she's learned the answer. "Surround yourself with the very best people in the business," she says. As examples of her best-person philosophy, she cites her co-star, director and costume designer. "Christopher Walken is one of this country's finest actors — period. He's added an element of mystery and strength to his character that makes this story very powerful." The producer/actress describes director Glenn Jordan as, "from an actor's point of view, arguably the most respected director working in television; he possesses a sensitivity that's extremely rare." As for costume designer Van Broughton Ramsey, "I loved his work in 'Lonesome Dove,' and I was confident he'd come up with wonderful, imaginative costumes for 'Sarah.' For me, when you do a period movie, your character isn't complete until you put on the clothes. They're tremendously important, and the costumes in 'Sarah' are superb."

# # #

TRUE STORY -- The HALLMARK HALL OF FAME presentation of "Sarah, Plain and Tall," airing on CBS Sunday, February 3, 1991, is based on Patricia MacLachlan's children's classic. MacLachlan says she wrote the Newbery Medal-winning book in 1985 as a gift for her mother. "She was suffering from the first stages of Alzheimer's," MacLachlan remembers, "and while she could still read I wanted to write something for her that would be very personal. Sarah, Plain and Tall is based on a true event in our family's history, when a mail-order bride came to Kansas from the East. This book meant a great deal to my mother -- and to me." In the HALLMARK HALL OF FAME presentation of "Sarah, Plain and Tall," Glenn Close plays the mail-order bride; Christopher Walken plays the widower, whose life she enriches.

# # #

FAMILY FIRST — The HALLMARK HALL OF FAME presentation of "Sarah, Plain and Tall," airing <u>Sunday, February 3, 1991</u> on CBS, stars Glenn Close and Christopher Walken. Close is Sarah, a woman from Maine who, in the early 1900s, answers a newspaper advertisement placed by a lonely Kansas widower, played by Christopher Walken. Walken's character has two children, played by Lexi Randall and Christopher Bell. "Sarah, Plain and Tall" marks the TV acting debut of 6-year-old Christopher Bell, although two of his three brothers, as well as his sister, are TV veterans. Michael, age 13, and David, 8, have appeared in several national and local (Minneapolis) commercials; their sister Andraya, 10, has worked in public television in Minneapolis. Ann Bell, the children's mother, says Christopher got interested in acting because the rest of the family was so busy. "His attitude," she says, "was, 'Everybody else is working, why can't I?'" Dublin-born Ann Bell says when it comes to acting, she's worked hard to promote a non-competitive atmosphere in her home. "My husband and I nip any notion of rivalry or jealousy in the bud," she says. "These children, including Christopher, are taught that above all else, your family is what's important." Christopher Bell was chosen from more than 1100 children who auditioned for the role of Caleb in "Sarah, Plain and Tall." How good an actor is he? Oscar-winner Christopher Walken says, "I could be Laurence Olivier in my scenes with him, and he'd still steal them. He's that good."

# # #

SURPRISE HIT -- The HALLMARK HALL OF FAME presentation of "Sarah, Plain and Tall," airing on CBS <u>Sunday, February 3, 1991</u>, is based on the best-selling book by Patricia MacLachlan. "Sarah" tells the story of a woman who journeys from Maine to Kansas in the early 1900s in response to a newspaper advertisement. MacLachlan, interviewed at her Massachusetts home, says when she was writing "Sarah" she never expected it would become a best-seller. "But it just seemed to touch a nerve with readers," she says. "It just seemed to connect. In the five years since it was published I've travelled all over the country speaking about it, and I've discovered that what people seem to like best is that it's such a hopeful story, in which good things happen to good people." More than one million copies of <u>Sarah, Plain and Tall</u> are in print. Glenn Close plays the title role in the HALLMARK HALL OF FAME presentation; Christopher Walken plays the widower whose life she enriches.

# # #

KANSAS LOCATION -- "Sarah, Plain and Tall," the HALLMARK HALL OF FAME presentation airing on CBS <u>Sunday, February 3, 1991</u>, was filmed on location in Kansas, most of it on a farm near Emporia belonging to John and Ada Bryan. "Sarah," starring Glenn Close and Christopher Walken, is based on Patricia MacLachlan's best-selling book which chronicles the life and times of a turn-of-the-century woman who moves to the Kansas prairie from her seacoast home in Maine. The Bryans have owned their 240-acre Kansas farm for 42 years. They lived in the farmhouse from 1948 to 1960; since then they've used the property as a hobby farm.

"We thought about selling it several times, but we just couldn't," says Ada Bryan. "Our three children would never have forgiven us. They love it here." The house was in "pretty rough shape," according to her husband, but a few years ago was rebuilt so it could be used for the filming of a feature that was to be called "The Last Cattle Drive." The picture was never made, but when location scouts for "Sarah, Plain and Tall" came upon it, they knew they'd found the perfect location for the HALLMARK HALL OF FAME production.

# # #

STEAM ENGINE -- Glenn Close and William Self, executive producers of the HALLMARK HALL OF FAME presentation of "Sarah, Plain and Tall," airing Sunday, February 3, 1991 on CBS, hoped to film the entire picture in Kansas and Maine. The story is based on Patricia MacLachlan's Newbery Medal-winning book about a turn-of-the-century woman from Maine who moves to Kansas in response to an ad placed by a lonely widower. "Kansas offered us everything we needed for the prairie scenes," says Self, "except for one very important thing: an authentic, steam-driven train." "Sarah" scouts found what they needed, though, at the Stuhr Museum in Grand Island, Nebraska. There was just one problem with the steam engine, built at the Baldwin Locomotive Works in 1908. It needed, in the words of Stuhr Museum assistant director Warren Rodgers, "extensive repairs" before its fires could be stoked. A timely contribution from the "Sarah, Plain and Tall" production company saved the day, however, and "Sarah" viewers will see Glenn Close (who, besides her producing chores, also plays the title role) alight from a train car and step into the period ambience of early-1900s prairie, artfully preserved at the Museum.

\# \# \#

AUTHOR MOVED -- The transformation of Patricia MacLachlan's children's classic, <u>Sarah, Plain and Tall</u>, from book to recording to television film was not an easy emotional experience for the Newbery Medal-winning author. The HALLMARK HALL OF FAME presentation of "Sarah, Plain and Tall," starring Glenn Close and Christopher Walken, airs on CBS <u>Sunday, February 3, 1991</u>. "When Glenn Close had finished reading the story for Caedmon Tapes, she invited me to the studio to hear it," MacLachlan remembers. "I put on earphones, and at the end of the first chapter I burst into tears, which were absolutely involuntary. Glenn breathed such life into my characters, they became real. She understood exactly what the story was about." "Sarah" is a woman from Maine who, in the early 1900s, journeys to Kansas in response to a newspaper ad placed by widower Jacob Witting (Walken). "The second time I burst into tears was on location during the filming in Kansas," MacLachlan says. "The actors gave heartbeats to my characters, which are based on real people and incidents in my family history. Watching the lives of my predecessors come to life before my very eyes was a profoundly moving experience."

\# \# \#

Press Contacts:

Stone/Hallinan Associates, Inc.
Los Angeles: 213/655-8970
New York: 212/489-5590

Hallmark Cards
Television Programming
816/274-8099

7449 MELROSE AVENUE, LOS ANGELES, CA 90046 (213) 655-8970   1350 AVENUE OF THE AMERICAS, NEW YORK, NY 10019 (212) 489-5590

Mark of Excellence
Presentations

Press Representative:
Owen Comora Associates
425 Madison Avenue
NY, NY 10017
Tel: 212/750-5556
Fax: 212/750-0183

ITEMS FOR 1990 'THE KENNEDY CENTER HONORS' TELECAST
A 'MARK OF EXCELLENCE PRESENTATION'
ON CBS-TV, FRIDAY, DEC. 28

WHAT HEPBURN SAID

Katharine Hepburn became the first Honoree in the 13-year history
of THE KENNEDY CENTER HONORS to speak after acknowledging a
standing ovation from the glittering, celebrity-packed audience.
The theater lights came up following a film tribute to her career
which included a scene from "Guess Who's Coming To Dinner" in
which she starred with Spencer Tracy. With tears in her eyes,
Ms. Hepburn leaned forward from her front row box seat and said
"I've never seen that scene with Spence before and I want to say
it was a privilege to work with such a wonderful actor. I was
very lucky to work with so many wonderful actors." Since they
were unexpected, her comments were not "miked" and, therefore,
not heard by most of those in attendance at the Kennedy Center
Opera House. THE KENNEDY CENTER HONORS will be telecast as A
MARK OF EXCELLENCE PRESENTATION, Friday, December 28 (9-11 p.m.,
ET) over the CBS Television Network.

CRONKITE'S DOUBLE

Ever since its inception, Walter Cronkite has been the host of
THE KENNEDY CENTER HONORS. Cronkite's stand-in for all thirteen
years has been Dave Gardner, of Vero Breach, Fl. Gardner is
practically a dead-ringer for Cronkite. Are there benefits
resulting from his near-celebrity status? "Sometimes I get a
good seat in a crowded restaurant," he said with a smile. There
are humorous moments, too. Recently, Cronkite looked at his
near-mirror image and said, "It's comforting to see you looking
so well this year." For the eighth consecutive year the telecast
will be a GM MARK OF EXCELLENCE PRESENTATION (Friday, December
28, 9-11 p.m., ET over the CBS Television Network).

THE BUCHWALDS' WORRIES

On 1990 THE KENNEDY CENTER HONORS telecast, humorist Art Buchwald
reveals how his family copes with the bad news they read in the
press; "What we do is assign each person in the family one thing
to worry about. My sister worries about Ivana Trump getting by
on $25,000,000 a year. My other sister worries about Leona
Helmsley doing a good job in Community Service. My wife worries
about Perrier getting into the drinking water -- and I worry all
the time about the Japanese buying out the Kennedy Center."
Meanwhile, THE KENNEDY CENTER HONORS will be telecast as a GM
MARK OF EXCELLENCE PRESENTATION, Friday, December 28, 9-11 p.m.,
ET over the CBS Television Network.

(more)

THE VOLUNTEERS

During the 13-year history of the prestigious KENNEDY CENTER
HONORS, volunteers have played a key behind-the-scenes role in
the production. This year approximately 120 local residents are
handling telephone calls, driving celebrities to and from
airports and racing from one end of the huge performing arts
complex to another escorting VIP's and whatever else needs doing.
No one has served longer than the mother-daughter team of Ruth
(mother) and Meryl Shapiro of Springfield, VA. They have been
volunteers every year since the HONORS were created. This year
they helped handle dressing room security for the stars. THE
KENNEDY CENTER HONORS will be telecast as a GM MARK OF EXCELLENCE
PRESENTATION on Friday, December 28, 9-11 p.m. over the CBS
Television Network.

A "MARK OF EXCELLENCE PRESENTATION"

For the eighth consecutive year, THE KENNEDY CENTER HONORS
telecast (Friday, Dec. 28 9-11 pm on CBS) will be fully-sponsored
by General Motors as one it's GM MARK OF EXCELLENCE
PRESENTATIONS. For the 1990-91 season, the HONORS program joins
an impressive array of quality television programs being shown
under that banner. Among the MARK OF EXCELLENCE PRESENTATIONS
already announced for this season (with more to come) are: LIVE
FROM LINCOLN CENTER, ALL OUR CHILDREN with Bill Moyers, a 90-
minute documentary examining America's youth in crisis; the July
repeat of THE CIVIL WAR (GM was the sole corporate underwriter of
the critically-praised, record-shattering, original telecast);
SEPARATE BUT EQUAL (A four-hour miniseries which will air on ABC
next spring), starring Sidney Poitier and Burt Lancaster; and
GENERAL MOTORS PLAYWRIGHTS THEATER, on A&E CAble Network.

A 'SWELL' PIECE OF EQUIPMENT

The mobile tv production truck (or control room) is the
electronic nerve center for THE KENNEDY CENTER HONORS telecast.
It's considered the 'Queen Mary' of them all. According to
engineer Tad Scripter, it's the best equipped mobile unit in the
world for musical extravaganzas because, among other things, it
contains a full 24 track audio recording system AND it can swell
from eight feet for travel to twelve feet when in use. THE
KENNEDY CENTER HONORS will be telecast as a GM MARK OF EXCELLENCE
PRESENTATION on Friday, December 28, 9-11 p.m. on the CBS
television network.

(more)

DOUBTING THOMAS

Veteran announcer, Tony Thomas, who has been doing THE KENNEDY CENTER HONORS since that show was first telecast in 1978, has just written a new book. "It's called ERROL FLYNN, THE SPY WHO NEVER WAS," he said. It refutes a book which came out a few years ago, claiming that Flynn had been a traitor and a Nazi spy. "I had known Flynn and had written about him before, so I thought it was time to put this nonsense to rest". THE KENNEDY CENTER HONORS will be telecast as a GM MARK OF EXCELLENCE PRESENTATION on CBS Television, Friday, December 28, 9-11 p.m.

STAR STUDDED "GREEN ROOM"

Before the beginning of the 1990 KENNEDY CENTER HONORS, the backstage area known as "the green room" looked like a performing arts hall of fame. Among those waiting patiently to "go on" to pay tribute to this year's honorees (Dizzy Gillespie, Katharine Hepburn, Rise Stevens, Jule Styne and Billy Wilder) were: Tyne Daly, Jack Jones, Hal Linden, Maureen McGovern, Tommy Tune, Ann Reinking, Jack Lemon, Walter Matthau, Walter Cronkite, Jerome Robbins, Lauren Bacall, Glenn Close, Angela Lansbury, Art Buchwald, Bill Cosby, Aprile Millo and Marilyn Horne. The KENNEDY CENTER HONORS will be telecast as a GM MARK OF EXCELLENCE PRESENTATION, Friday, December 28, 9-11 p.m., ET over the CBS Television Network.

SINGING STAND-IN

Annette Poulard, of Washington, DC, is an unusual stand-in. For THE KENNEDY CENTER HONORS, she's hired to stand-in for the likes of Leontyne Price, Roberta Peters, Maureen McGovern and Marilyn Horne. But unlike most stand-ins, she also sings the stars' roles during the rehearsal. Annette is a trained operatic singer and producer, who has even performed in her own musical production at The Kennedy Center. For the eighth consecutive year, General Motors will sponsor THE KENNEDY CENTER HONORS telecast as one of its GM MARK OF EXCELLENCE PRESENTATIONS. It will be telecast on the CBS Television Network, Friday, December 28, 9 -11 p.m., ET.

#-#-#-#

December, 1990

7

PHOTOS & CAPTIONS

Δ **There are three basic ways of captioning photos: there's the clip-on caption, the strip-on caption, and the print-on caption.**

Δ **The clip-on caption** consists of a piece of paper that is clipped (taped or glued) to the photo. The caption contains the program information, identifying information about the subject matter of the photos, and some descriptive language of how the two relate to each other. Whether you can see the picture and read the caption at the same time depends on how the paper is folded and attached. If the caption is taped or glued on the back, you must turn the photo over to either read the caption or see the picture.

These kind of captions take extra time to attach. They may get separated and lost from the photo. They may also increase the cost of postage. However, if there is a mistake or change, they are easier and less costly to replace.

Δ **The strip-on caption** is placed on the bottom of the photo when the photo is printed. This caption becomes a permanent part of the photo. It cuts down on the cost of labor and postage.   You can read the caption and see the picture at the same time. However, if there is a mistake or change, all the photos must be dumped and redone.

Δ **The print-on caption** is applied *after* a photo has been developed and printed. It is photocopied onto the back of a photo. This is done at a quick-print shop, rather than in a photo lab. You must run a test first, to make sure the caption does not show through on the front of the photo. You should also discuss this with the photo lab, so it will use the right kind of paper for your photos. The print-on caption cuts down on office time (your staff does not have to tape on captions) and the cost of postage. However, you must turn the photo over to either read the caption or see the photo. Also, if there are mistakes or changes, you must either write in the corrections by hand or print a "Change" or "Correction" under the caption, which requires another print run. When we eliminated the clip-on caption at NBC, we went to this type of caption (please see the "Remington Steele" example which follows).

One of the problems with "permanent" captions is that you may not have fully confirmed information about airdate and time when you could already be printing your photos. You don't want to take a chance by using uncertain information. The question then becomes one of production logistics: How long can you wait until you must get your photos printed?

CLIP-ONS

"Sarah, Plain and Tall" photos have clip-on captions. Note the use of a slug-line: PRAIRIE FAMILY -- , GLENN CLOSE STARS --. Note also how these captions provide the editor (and reader) with full information about the people in the photo, the particular show, the network, airdate and time, and the series. This places all the essential information at an editor's fingertips. The caption may get cut down, but at least editors don't have to scramble through a press kit for missing information or place a frantic call to a publicist. It is also possible that an editor may want to run the caption in full, particularly if there will be no accompanying story. It is advisable to place contact information on your caption, just as you do on other copy. It's always best to double-space these captions, as seen here.

STRIP-ONS

"Wings" photos used a strip-on caption, consisting of three parts: the show logo, a one-line caption identifying the actor and the character he plays, and five lines of copyright information, in small type.

"LifeStories" also used a strip-on caption. It, too, consists of three parts: the show logo, the copyright information, and a full caption. It contains the name of the network and points out that the photos tie in with the premiere episode of the series. However, we are not given a broadcast date or time. Why? There may be a number of reasons:

- The photo may have been sent out to the media months before, as part of an advance publicity campaign, when the premiere episode was known, but the airdate was not.

- The photos had to be printed before the airdate was known. It was better to print the photos and mail them out, than to wait till the last minute. This way editors could be notified by fax, phone, or electronic newsletter of the airdate and they could then activate the photos that they had on hand.

Did you notice that the caption refers to two photos? That's because there are two photos, printed side by side, horizontally, each photo taking up half of the 8x10 space. Two photos printed this way are called a "two-up." If you had four head shots, for instance, you could do a "four-up." "Two-ups," "three-ups" and "four-ups" are particularly good to use when you want to show a sequence, such as an actor undergoing a makeup transformation (before, during, and after). If your images are going to get too small, don't go this route. It's better then to use individual 8x10 photos.

Be sure to always identify everyone in a photo (full name and character). If you decide to include the names of other major stars in the show, who are not shown in the picture, be sure to make that clear:

The show stars Jane Terrific as Mrs. Wonderful (left), opposite Joe Fabulous as mean Mr. Nogood (not pictured), in this drama about, etc.....Seen here also are (and then names/characters of others in the photo).

Make sure an editor and reader will always be able to tell who's who (left to right; center; standing, seated; front row, back row, or whatever else will do the trick).

PRINT-ONS

Check the **"Remington Steele"** caption. It also serves as an example of how a "revision" is handled. It is a good idea to always date captions (using the date the photo is being mailed out) and to use any other kind of keys that let you know who the photo was mailed to (this particular photo went to several mailing lists, as indicated by the letters under the caption).

Sarah
P L A I N   A N D   T A L L

SUNDAY, FEBRUARY 3, 1991

PRAIRIE FAMILY -- THE HALLMARK HALL OF FAME, television's longest-running and most distinguished series, begins its 40th anniversary year <u>Sunday, February 3, 1991 at 9 p.m. ET</u> with the presentation on CBS of SARAH, PLAIN AND TALL. The heartwarming story of a mail-order bride in the early 1900s is based on the Newbery Medal-winning children's classic by Patricia MacLachlan, who adapted it for television with Carol Sobieski. Sarah Wheaton, played by Glenn Close, leaves her Maine seacoast home and moves to the Kansas prairie, where she enters the lives of two motherless children, played by (l-r) Lexi Randall and Christopher Bell, and their lonely father, played by Christopher Walken. The 168th presentation of THE HALLMARK HALL OF FAME is directed by Glenn Jordan ("Promise," "Home Fires Burning") and was filmed on location in Kansas and Maine.

Sarah

PLAIN AND TALL

SUNDAY, FEBRUARY 3, 1991

GLENN CLOSE STARS -- Glenn Close plays the title role in SARAH, PLAIN AND TALL, the 168th presentation of THE HALLMARK HALL OF FAME, airing on CBS Sunday, February 3, 1991 at 9 p.m. ET. Based on the Newbery Medal-winning children's classic, SARAH, PLAIN AND TALL is the heartwarming story of a mail-order bride in the early 1900s. Sarah, played by Glenn Close, leaves the serenity and security of her Maine seacoast home and moves to the rolling hills of the Kansas prairie, where she enters the lives of two motherless children and their lonely father, Jacob, who is played by Christopher Walken. SARAH, PLAIN AND TALL launches the fortieth anniversary year of television's longest-running and most-honored series: THE HALLMARK HALL OF FAME.

WINGS

Thomas Haden Church as Lowell Mather

Left photo: Lindsay Crouse stars as Rebecca McManus in the premiere episode of **LIFESTORIES**, a one-hour dramatic anthology series on NBC. Crouse portrays a woman in her forties who is desperate to have a baby. Vowing to do whatever it takes to overcome her conception problems, she experiences high-risk in-vitro fertilization and ultimately, in-utero surgery. *Right photo*: Lindsay Crouse and Dwight Schultz star as Rebecca McManus and Steve Arnold, a childless couple desperately trying to conceive, in the premiere episode of **LIFESTORIES**, a one-hour dramatic anthology series on NBC.

LIFESTORIES

NBC Photo

Press Department 30 Rockefeller Plaza New York, N.Y. 10020

THRUST AND PARRY — Remington (Pierce Brosnan, right) draws upon his swashbuckling fencing talents and love of old movies when he finds himself sparring with a determined combatant (Barrie Ingham), in the "Scene Steelers" episode of "Remington Steele," NBC-TV's romantic comedy-mystery series, Tuesday, Nov. 1 (9-10 p.m. NYT).

(10/7/83)

(A)(B)(C)(D) (SFP 1&2)

ATTENTION PHOTO EDITORS:

The "Scene Steelers" episode of "Remington Steele" will be telecast Tuesday, Nov. 15 (9-10 p.m. NYT), which revises the information contained in the above photo caption.

135

8

THE PITCH LETTER
&
COVER LETTER

Pitch letters and cover letters are kissing cousins if not identical twins. The difference is subtle.

Press kits normally contain a generic letter alerting the recipient to what you are publicizing and what's in the press kit. The letter lists major points of interest about the event. It lets an editor know what else is available, upon request (if you did not send it): color transparencies, a tape of the show, an electronic press kit, and possible interviews with the stars. You invite the editor to call you about whatever else he or she needs. That's a cover letter.

A pitch letter is more specific. It is aimed at a particular person and at a particular outlet. It seeks to suggest one or more angles of interest to that individual and outlet. It is often sent by itself, to test the waters. A follow-up phone call determines whether there is interest. If so, you may be asked to send additional materials (a press kit, show tape, or B-roll, or all of the above). Finally, the editor or producer/talent coordinator will tell you that they're interested in your event and that they want to do an interview or place your star on their program.

In short, the difference between a cover letter and a pitch letter is the difference between saying, "Here's a great great restaurant -- I hope you'll try it" and "Here's a great restaurant -- how about having lunch?"

Even though pitch letters are aimed at particular individuals and outlets, I have found that you don't have to start from scratch every time. I create one letter for print media and one for broadcast media. A personal note, and a little fine tuning, will usually take care of the rest.

Again, keep in mind, that the only difference sometimes between a cover letter and a pitch letter is that one is generic ("Dear Editor," or, "Dear Media Person") and the other is addressed to a specific individual at a specific media outlet.

Finally, it must be said that not everyone uses a cover letter when doing a mass mailing of press kits. You need to be guided here by your company's policy and the particular situation.

Δ **A word or two about phone pitching.** Should you or shouldn't you pitch by phone? There is no simple answer. Everything you say on this subject needs to be qualified.

There are a number of good reasons for first getting on the phone. To begin with, if you haven't talked to the person within the last 24 hours, call and find out of the person is still there and in that particular job. People get sick, go on vacation, are given new positions, and are hired or fired. You don't want to send something to someone who isn't there or who turns out to be the wrong person. You can lose valuable time that way, which can make a difference between making a deadline and missing it. Also, if in doubt, ask who you should be dealing with.

So call and check. If you don't manage to reach the person, check with a live receptionist (if you can find your way to one through the voice mail maze).

If you do reach the person, there are several courtesies to consider.
   √ Identify yourself quickly.
   √ Ask if the person is on deadline, or if you could have one or two minutes of their time. If they have a minute or two, proceed to your pitch. If not, ask when you might call back.
   √ The pitch should be brief and focused. This is not the time to start figuring out your angle. You must have everything well in mind. Don't take advantage of your two minutes and go 10 minutes, unless the media person has questions and encourages you to talk further.

Invariably, you will be asked to "send something in writing," if the media person is interested or even half-way interested (or you can offer to do so, if there is an element of doubt). If the person says to fax him something, don't fax the whole press kit! Fax the pitch letter, and maybe one other thing (a bio, a fact sheet, or some highlights). If the person wants a press kit and maybe a tape of the show and some B-roll, get it there fast: by messenger, by priority mail, or by overnight delivery. Strike while the interest is there.

Another reason to call ahead is simply to alert the individual that you are "faxing something" or "sending something." Some editors don't like this, but in most cases you only get their answering machines anyway, so just leave a message.

The best justification for calling is time or topicality. If your story involves some fast-breaking news, or a tie-in with something that is in the news, you need to contact the media quickly. Or, one of your stars, who was not available to you before, has suddenly become available. Where time is of the essence, don't stand on ceremony. Pick up the phone and explain the reason for calling, rather than writing, first.

You will still be asked to "send something," but at least you will get a quick reaction and be able to work with maximum efficiency.

Now let's take a look at some pitch letters.

PRINT When it comes to model pitch letters, you can't do any better than to study those prepared by Carol Stevens & Associates.

"Santa Let's look at the one sent to Joe Stein, the television editor of the
Barbara" *San Diego Tribune*. It is obvious from the first paragraph that the writer had made prior phone contact with Stein (a phone pitch).

In her letter to Stein, Lori Miller quickly reiterates what had been discussed in the phone call: Bridget and Jerome Dobson, the creators and headwriters of the daytime drama, "Santa Barbara," have a fascinating story.

She gives a reason why this story is newsworthy: the husband and wife team has just returned to the show after a three-year absence.

She says all that succinctly in the first paragraph. But the real angle -- the human interest factor -- is to be found in the second paragraph (which is really still part of the first paragraph): The Dobsons are risk takers -- their own marriage and fascinating lifestyle have direct bearing on the storylines and characters of the show.

That's intriguing. It leads you to wonder how much of their own life is reflected in all the juicy goings-on of this soap opera. The editor is being invited to take his readers behind the scenes for an intimate, revealing look.

Miller strengthens the pitch by indicating what changes are being planned and then lists some other "interesting facts."

Note how easy it is to read this letter and how the "interesting facts" are highlighted by using short, indented paragraphs.

The writer lets the editor know that she will call him in a few days, or that he should feel free to call her (and she provides the phone number at this point for his convenience).

This letter -- personally addressed in each case -- went to newspaper editors in the top 50 markets.

BROADCAST Another excellent example of a pitch letter customized
MEDIA to the needs of a particular media outlet is the one to Debbie DiMaio, executive producer of the "Oprah Winfrey" show.

A good pitch letter captures the essence of the story in the first paragraph, or better yet, in the first sentence. The first sentence here is a grabber! It asks: "How many people have the opportunity to 'play God?'"

I defy anyone to stop reading at this point. You can't. Quickly we are told: "Bridget and Jerome Dobson do (this) on a daily basis!"

The writer then lists their credentials to establish credibility, mentions the popularity of soap operas, and then suggests that the Dobsons could give Oprah's audience and viewers a provocative look at the makings of a soap opera.

She further suggests that the Dobsons will give viewers a look at their own marriage and lifestyle, and the bearing these have on the series.

Having made these claims, Miller now supports them with specifics, using bullets to mark each point (I like the use of bullets -- they let you get your points across quickly and they make reading easy, like a fact sheet).

Take a look at the next to the last paragraph. It's a very interesting paragraph from a PR point of view. We learn that the Dobsons will be in the Chicago area in June. Why is this mentioned here and not in the first paragraph? When you write, keep your reader's state of mind and mental process in mind. Pitch letters are read with lightning speed. Editors, producers, talent coordinators have to make snap judgments. Key words can trigger a "yes" or a "no." If your first or second paragraph states, "the Dobsons will be in the Chicago area in June," you might kill the deal right there, if the talk show is already booked for that month. The producer may not read beyond that sentence. You first want to intrigue the producer so much that he or she will want your client. If the producer can't book your client when he or she is in town, the producer may offer you a different date. If the show is important enough, your client may be more than willing to make another trip. If, however, your client is only available for a limited time, do mention that in the beginning of your letter. In this case, June would have been most convenient, but the Dobsons would have made themselves available at some other time.

Take a look at another sentence: "The Dobsons could appear as solo guests, or with other soap opera writing teams and stars." This is a clever sentence and placed just where it should be. What's the point of that sentence? Why is it placed here and not near the beginning of the letter?

What the publicist has done here -- and done well -- is build the strongest case possible for her client. You hope that the print media will then do a full story on your client or, in the case of the broadcast media, that the show will devote a whole program or segment to your client only!

However, if it becomes a question of all or nothing, and the answer might be "nothing," you want to have a fall-back position. If you're dealing with print media, you would suggest a "roundup story," which, in this case, would mean involving other soap operas. In the case of broadcast media, it would mean suggesting a "theme" show, involving "other soap opera writing teams and stars."

Again, you don't want to suggest that up front in your letter, if you think you have a chance to have it all. Since Oprah is most likely to handle this as a theme show, do let the producer know that your client would be receptive. The point of that sentence is to suggest another way to go with the show or to indicate that the client is agreeable to appearing with others.

Δ **Regional publication.** Let's look at a third pitch letter from Carol Stevens & Associates, also written by Lori Miller. This one is to Judith Woodburn at the *Milwaukee Monthly*.

Read the first paragraph. What are the three magic words? That's right, "native of Milwaukee." If you're dealing with a local paper, you must look for a local angle; if you're dealing with a regional publication, you must look for a regional angle.

Miller establishes her client's credibility quickly: the Dobsons are the creators and head writers of the Emmy-award winning daytime drama, "Santa Barbara."

Check how Miller strengthens the regional story with fascinating, solid family information (third and fourth paragraphs).

These three pitch letters -- about the same client -- are excellent because the writer has taken the trouble to gather concrete information and then customize it to the totally different needs of the three media outlets involved.

The principles of writing an effective pitch letter are very simple:
- Bring the essence of your story into focus in your first sentence or paragraph in an arresting, intriguing, provocative or humorous way.
- Support your claim, your story. What makes it newsworthy? What gives your client credibility? What are the elements of the story, the highlights?

The principles are simple, but the execution takes skill.

Δ **Celebrity pitch letter.** For an example of a celebrity pitch letter, take a look at the one from Baker • Winokur • Ryder Public Relations promoting their client, **Mariette Hartley**. The letter, sent to Hank Rieger, editor/publisher of *EMMY Magazine,* calls attention to four areas of interest: Hartley's new TV series, her highly acclaimed memoirs published by Putnam Books, her illustrious career, and her humanitarian activities. This letter was obviously sent with a biography, and other materials, that would provide additional details.

MEDIA TOUR   I would like to share a personal experience here involving media pitching. One of my accounts is the National Geographic Television office which opened on the West Coast in Studio City, California in 1991. My responsibilities are primarily to create awareness of the office in the entertainment community. The P.R. people with the Television Division of the National Geographic Society, located in Washington, D.C., and Ketchum Public Relations, in New York, handle the programming publicity (in association with whoever is broadcasting the programs).

When the Public Relations Department of the National Geographic Television Division decided to give one of its Specials a special PR push, they brought in the Washington, D.C. based Devillier Communications agency and me to work with them and Ketchum P.R.

The program was "Eternal Enemies: Lions and Hyenas," to be broadcast on PBS January 22, 1992. It was a remarkable documentary, filmed by the highly regarded husband and wife team of Dereck and Beverly Joubert, who live and work in the African bush for months at a time. In November and December of 1991, there had been some preliminary discussion about bringing them to the U.S. for a West Coast and East Coast media tour.

On Tuesday, January 7, I received a call from the National Geographic office in Washington, D.C., that a decision had been made to bring the Jouberts over here for a three-city media tour: New York, Washington, D.C., and Los Angeles. The Jouberts would arrive in Los Angeles Sunday, January 12. Could I set up media for them? I would have them here three days: Monday through Wednesday, January 13 to 15.

Ketchum PR would handle the print media in New York and Devillier Communications would handle the broadcast media in New York and Washington, D.C., and National Geographic would handle the print media in Washington, D.C.

I had at my disposal an excellent press kit, a tape of the show, black and white photos of the Jouberts on location, and 3/4" B-roll, including clips from the show, footage showing the Jouberts working on location in Botswana, and interviews with them. I also had an excellent pitch letter to work with.

The following pitch letter represents a collaborative effort by Ketchum Public Relations (NY), Devillier Communications (Washington, D.C.) and National Geographic Specials/Television Division/Public Relations (Washington, D.C.)

Dear   :

An adventurous husband and wife filmmaking team redefine the term "job stress."

For filmmakers Beverly and Dereck Joubert, working in the African bush is risky business. Imagine being charged by a male lion on your way to work or having your bus turned over by an elephant. How would you explain to your boss that wild hyenas destroyed the project you were working on? And what would you do if a herd of buffalo, fleeing from lions, raced through your office?

The Jouberts, who've spent the last 10 years of their lives filming in wildest Africa, have experienced it all -- and lived to tell about it. Now this fascinating duo, ranked among the foremost wildlife filmmakers in the world, is coming to the U.S. on behalf of their latest project, the new National Geographic Special, ETERNAL ENEMIES: LIONS AND HYENAS, airing on PBS, Wednesday, January 22 at 8 p.m. ET (check local listings).

In a film that pushes the bounds of wildlife documentaries, the Jouberts have exposed the harsh realities of life in the wild and captured the bitter rivalry between two natural enemies -- African lions and hyenas. For a millenia, these two species have waged a war that goes beyond mere competition for food and territory. If animals could hate, this is what it would look like.

Most lion and hyena activity takes place at night, making it almost impossible to film. But by slowly acclimating the animals to the bright lights, the Jouberts were able to capture this startling, real life drama on film. In fact, their primary research into lion and hyena behavior has now debunked many myths about both species.

Enclosed is information on the Jouberts and the extraordinary National Geographic Special, ETERNAL ENEMIES: LIONS AND HYENAS. We believe you will find this remarkable filmmaking team -- their perilous lifestyle, approach to filmmaking and plans for the future -- fascinating and hope you'll consider featuring them in an interview. They will be in the U.S. and available for interviews beginning the week of January 13th.

I'll be in touch shortly to discuss the Jouberts with you. In the meantime, please feel free to call me at (phone number) with any questions.

Best regards,

Note how this letter is true to form. It starts with an attention-getting statement that captures the essence of the story. The second paragraph then provides some intriguing, factual examples that support the story. Good pitch letters, like this one, let selective, tell-tale facts, not flowery adjectives, make their point.

Now that you have the editor's rapt attention, you must provide the justification for the story. That happens here in the third paragraph where the editor is told that the Jouberts have a show coming up on PBS, that they are coming to the U.S., and that they will be available for interviews.

Professional writing is not a hit-or-miss affair. Every word must be carefully thought out and chosen. Note how this is true here, for instance, in the way credibility is established with a few well chosen words: **The Jouberts, who've spent the last 10 years of their lives filming in wildest Africa... (are) ranked among the foremost wildlife filmmakers in the world....**

The letter then provides additional points of interest, describing the nature of the program. It also points out that the Jouberts have uncovered new information about lions and hyenas, debunking long-held myths.

When this letter was drafted, no one knew when the Jouberts would be available in any of the three cities. Once I got those dates for the Los Angeles area, I modified the letter accordingly. I also spelled out the materials that were available.

The Jouberts had been in Los Angeles the previous year for post production on their show. At the time I had been asked to make some limited media contacts. In addition to my own pitch letter, I had prepared a list of highlights about their life and work. I now brought those highlights up to date and used them as well.

DERECK & BEVERLY JOUBERT
National Geographic Filmmakers

HIGHLIGHTS

-- **THIRTYSOMETHING**: The attractive husband & wife team are both in their early thirties

-- **MAJOR CREDITS**: Their National Geographic credits include "Journey to the Forgotten River," "Elephant," "The Stolen River," and "The Long Night of the Lion"

-- **PROGRAM COMING UP**: "Eternal Enemies: Lions and Hyenas," a new National Geographic Special, Jan. 22 at 8 p.m . ET, PT on PBS nationally (KCET Channel 28 in Los Angeles).
In the Savuti region of northern Botswana, lions and spotted hyenas share overlapping territories and often prey on the same food sources. For centuries, these two mortal enemies have waged a vicious blood feud that goes far beyond competition for food. If animals could hate, this is what it might look like.

Says Dereck: 'Occasionally if the lions kill something and their attention is all focused on the meat, I will use the steadicam, run out from the vehicle and get that extra touch of cross-lighting. At times I was within 10 feet of the lions, about 50 feet from the safety of the truck. I only do this when I know that all the lions of the pride are already in, and not lurking in the dark behind me somewhere."

Says Beverly: "On one occasion we spent three weeks working on a new clan of hyenas that were totally unaccustomed to lights or vehicles. They had a large kill and night after night we sat with them, gradually moving in closer and closer and putting soft lights on them for longer and longer spells. For the first two weeks Dereck didn't roll the camera. After that, we could work with them without any fear of interference or affected behavior."

PRIMARY RESEARCH: The couple's field research uncovers new behavioral information that debunks some of the myths about lions and hyenas. The Jouberts follow key individuals in the lion pride and hyena clan, guiding viewers through the complex behavior of these two natural enemies. Their primary research into lion and hyena behavior has helped to dispel many myths about both species: hyenas are proven to be capable hunters as well as scavengers; lions will scavenge hyena kills as well as hunt down prey; and a hyena clan that outnumbers a lion pride can overpower the big cats to win the spoils of a kill. The Jouberts have filmed difficult to get, incredible, never-before-seen footage, much of it shot at night.

144

-- GETTING ALONG IN THE BUSH (husband-wife): The Jouberts are unusually close, rarely spending much time away from one another; it's a matter of survival. "You eventually become one person in a way, you're so bonded together," says Beverly. "Most of the time we have to sleep in that vehicle and in the morning you climb over the front seats and there you are, you carry on. In a situation with lions, you're not going to get out of the vehicle too often."
They have also learned to communicate. "It's the only way to solve problems out there," she said. "If you're feeling terrible or you don't want to talk to one another, it's better to say, 'It's not your fault, but I'm in a bad mood so you must leave me alone.'"

-- SEX IN AFRICA (lions & hyenas):
Even though lions may mate more than a hundred times in one week of courtship, lionesses are known to have a very low success rate in becoming pregnant.
Early observers thought that hyenas were hermaphrodites -- animals of dual sex. While spotted hyenas have nearly identical genitalia, they are indeed either male or female.
Lions are social and affectionate -- young lions enjoy rubbing faces with adults. By the age of three or four, male lions are sexually mature.
Male hyenas are submissive to the ruling females.
Hyenas are not related to dogs but cats -- they are distant cousins of the mongoose, a member of the cat family.

-- HOW THE JOUBERTS GET THEIR STORIES: The couple's proximity to the action makes it possible for them to track animals over months and even years, which, as one writer said, creates "individual stories for the film that inject a dramatic tension not often found in wildlife documentaries."

-- DIVISION OF LABOR: He does the photography, she does the sound and stills.

-- HOW THEY LIVE: They live in a tent; a second tent is their editing room, with a generator for their editing machine; they have a small bilge pump, water purification device, and a shower Dereck rigged up using nearby river water; when they go into the bush to film, they live in their Land Cruiser, carrying their own water and often cooking on the vehicle's manifold.

-- TAKING RISKS: They have been charged by male lions; an elephant pushed over their tent when they were not in it and another upended their modified Toyota Land Cruiser when they were in it; hyenas got into their film storage container and scattered rolls about; buffalos, fleeing from lions, ran into their vehicle; crocodiles routinely wait patiently to spring at them along the river.

(more)

-- **PATIENCE**: They are patient, spending days waiting for the right shots; because they allowed lions to become used to the lights they must occasionally use, one of their shows includes extraordinary night shots.

-- **FILMING RULE**: They cling to one tenet: Do not interfere with the animals' behavior (even when an animal is in danger).

-- **HOURS FROM TOWN**: When they filmed in Botswana, they were five hours' drive (one hour by helicopter) from Kasane, the nearest town; they depend on a radio phone for communication and a medication book and a stash of medication, including painkillers and anti-malaria tablets, for emergencies. On the lions/hyenas Special, they were 1000 miles away from a plug point, lighting supply or any camera technicians.

--**POTENTIAL HEALTH DANGER**: a new strain of malaria that attacks the brain. Says Beverly: "I think you have about four days if you don't get treatment before you die."

--**CLOSE CALL**: Dereck once went to check on a rhinoceros carcass that was stuck, and became stuck himself; his wife, thinking it was funny, grabbed her camera, but when he announced that he was sinking, she realized the seriousness of the situation; 'If Beverly threw a cable out and attached it to the vehicle and pulled me, it would have cracked my legs, the mud was so thick," said Dereck. Instead, she threw him a shovel, while his arms were still free, and he had to dig his own way out. "If I'd been there by myself, I would have been in trouble."

-- **CIVILIZATION**: "We don't fit in very well in cities," says Beverly. "We don't know much about how to dress and act, and we always think, 'Why is everybody looking at us?' Civilization seems fantastically noisy to us. Where we live you often have to listen carefully to hear any sound at all."

-- **WORD POLLUTION** : Talking about Los Angeles Dereck says: "In the restaurants we could hear what everybody was saying, even all the way across the room. (There is so much) word pollution. Where we live, words are important. Words are what you write down on a piece of paper and send to somebody, and he reads them, and it matters. Here, we walk down the street and there are words everywhere. So many signs, and we feel we have to read them all. It takes us forever to get anywhere."

CONTACT: Rolf Gompertz, Rolf Gompertz Communications, 818/9?9-3576

146

In several instances, the editor or producer/talent coordinator just wanted something sent by fax at first. In those cases, I sent the pitch letter and the highlights. Once there was interest, the media asked for the rest of the material. The print media received the press kit, a tape of the show, and black and white photos. The broadcast media (radio) received the press kit only. The TV outlets were sent the press kit, a tape of the show, and B-roll.

The results were gratifying for all three cities. In Los Angeles, I placed the Jouberts on Entertainment Tonight, syndicated to 184 markets, and KABC Talkradio's "Peter Tilden Show." The TV writer/critic for the *Orange County Register* wrote a full-page story for the Sunday supplement, using two of our black and white photos. The science writer of the *Los Angeles Times* wrote a major piece that ran on the front page of the *Calendar* section and which was continued on two pages inside. The article was accompanied by a two-column photo of the Jouberts, shot by a *Times* photographer.

Other placements included:

PRINT
Washington Post (per National Geographic's PR Department); *Boston Globe* (per Ketchum); *New York Daily News* (per Ketchum); *North Jersey Herald & News* (per Ketchum).

WIRES & SYNDICATES
Reuters (per Devillier); *Gannett News Service* (per Ketchum)

TELEVISION
"Sonya Live"/CNN (per Devillier); WUSA-TV/9/CBS (per Devillier)

RADIO
"First Light"/NBC Radio (per Devillier); "Daily Edition"/Monitor Radio (per Devillier); "Harden & Weaver"/WMAL-AM (per Devillier); NBC Radio News (per WETA-TV); "Voice of America" (per WETA-TV); "PM"/WETA Radio (per WETA-TV).

There's a moral to this story: you don't have be Madonna to get media attention. If you have an interesting client, a good story and the right pitch, you can get some great media coverage.

The show did well in the ratings and made the list of the 25 most popular shows in PBS history.

April 3, 1991

Mr. Joe Stein
Television Editor
SAN DIEGO TRIBUNE
350 Camino de la Reina
San Diego, CA 92108

Dear Joe:

It was a pleasure speaking with you about Bridget and Jerome Dobson, the creators and headwriters of the daytime drama, SANTA BARBARA. As I mentioned, the Dobsons recently returned to the show after a three-year absence -- and now serve as the headwriters and creative production executives.

Creative risk-taking has been a hallmark of the Dobsons. And, their own marriage and fascinating lifestyle are strong role models for the show's look and characters.

The Dobsons have planned a variety of changes for the seasons. Character changes are at the top of the list. These include "Mason," portrayed by Gordon Thompson (Adam Carrington of "Dynasty"). Bridget Dobson says she will turn his character around with 10 days of psychologically riveting material.

Changes are also slated for lead characters "Gina," played by Robin Mattson and "Kelly," played by Carrington Garland.

Other interesting facts about the Dobsons, include:

-   In most of the country, SANTA BARBARA airs opposite both "General Hospital" and "Guiding Light," shows for which the Dobsons were once headwriters. So the characters they're writing about now are competing with characters from their past.

-   Bridget Dobson is the second in a daytime drama dynasty. Her mother, Doris Hursley, created "General Hospital," and her daughter, Mary, has written for SANTA BARBARA.

-   Their ten-year residence in Santa Barbara is the basis of the series.

148

-   Although the show has been awarded the Emmy for the past three years as Outstanding Daytime Drama, the ratings have dropped since the Dobsons left the show in 1987. Now that they have returned, will viewers return as well?

-   The show will celebrate its seventh anniversary in July. Could this be lucky 7 for SANTA BARBARA?

I am confident that they can give you a warm and provocative interview, when you are ready to discuss the "behind the scenes" of the show.

I am forwarding background material on the Dobsons and the show for your review. I will call you in a few days. Or, feel free to call me at (213) 271-5557.

I look forward to speaking with you again soon.

Best,

Lori E. Miller

CAROL STEVENS
& ASSOCIATES
PUBLIC RELATIONS

May 3, 1991

Ms. Debbie DiMaio
Executive Producer
OPRAH WINFREY
Harpo Productions
110 N. Carpenter
Chicago, IL 60607

Dear Debbie:

How many people have the opportunity to "play God?" To control the destiny of an entire city? To decide who lives and who dies -- who will marry and who will divorce?

Bridget and Jerome Dobson do on a daily basis!

Every day Bridget and Jerome put pen to paper and create and shape the lives of the fictional characters in the daytime drama SANTA BARBARA.

The Dobsons are the creators of SANTA BARBARA and recently returned to the Emmy-award winning show as the head writers.

For more than 50 years, the soap opera genre has captured the imagination and hearts of millions of devoted fans who live vicariously through the exploits of their favorite soap characters.

I would like to suggest Bridget and Jerome Dobson as guests on the Oprah Winfrey show. The Dobsons can provide your audience with a very provocative, behind-the-scenes look at the making of a daytime soap. They can also offer insight in the psyche of the characters and what makes these heros and villains so addictive.

You will also discover that their marriage and lifestyle are strong role models for the show's glamorous look and the lives of the characters who inhabit the series.

There are so many intriguing aspects to the Dobsons' lives.

- Bridget Dobson is the second in a soap writing dynasty. Her mother, Doris Hursley, created "General Hospital" and her daughter, Mary (a Chicago resident), has written for SANTA BARBARA.

150

- It is interesting to note, that Bridget's mother and father got their start in Chicago, writing for a local radio soap opera.

- The Dobsons have been head writers for other long-running, hit shows, including the "Guiding Light" and "General Hospital."

- Does a couple responsible for the writing of hundreds of pages of script every week, 52 weeks a year, have a private life, or is much being revealed on the screen?

The Dobsons will be in the Chicago area in June, a month prior to SANTA BARBARA's seventh anniversary. This might be an ideal time to schedule an appearance. The Dobsons could appear as solo guests, or with other soap opera writing teams and stars.

I am forwarding some background material for your review and consideration. I'll give you a call in a few days to determine your interest. Or, feel free to call me at (213) 271-5557.

Best,

Lori E. Miller

encl.

April 15, 1991

Ms. Judith Woodburn
Features
MILWAUKEE MONTHLY
312 E. Buffalo
Milwaukee, WI 53202

Dear Judith:

I am writing to you regarding a native of Milwaukee whose life and personal experiences have been the basis and foundation for an Emmy-award winning daytime drama.

Bridget Dobson, along with her husband Jerome, created the soap, SANTA BARBARA. In addition to being the show's creators, the Dobsons also serve as head writers for SANTA BARBARA.

Bridget was born in Milwaukee and her family has a rich and interesting history in the Milwaukee area. Her parents, Doris and Frank Hursley created the soap GENERAL HOSPITAL. Prior to their writing careers, Doris Hursley was a lawyer in the Milwaukee area and Frank Hursley served as the Chairman of the English department with the University of Wisconsin.

Bridget's grandfather, Victor Berger, was also the first socialist Congressman in Wisconsin. Her grandfather's professional notes and papers were recently donated by the family to the University of Wisconsin.

Bridget Dobson has a wealth of information and anecdotes to share regarding her family's history and her work with SANTA BARBARA.

I am forwarding some background material on the Dobsons for your review. I will call you in a few days to determine your interest in developing a feature piece on Bridget. Or, feel free to call me at (213) 271-5557.

I look forward to speaking with you soon.

Sincerely,

Lori E. Miller

9304 CIVIC CENTER DRIVE, SUITE   BEVERLY HILLS, CA 90210

TEL. (213) 271-5557   FAX (213) 278-6242

BAKER · WINOKUR · RYDER
P U B L I C   R E L A T I O N S

Beverly Hills • New York

January 7, 1991

Hank Rieger
EMMY MAGAZINE
3500 West Olive Ave #700
Burbank, Ca 91505

Dear Hank,

The Fall of 1990 promises to be a busy time for Emmy Award-
winning actress **Mariette Hartley**. In addition to returning to
network television in the starring role of news producer 'Liz
McVay' on the new CBS-TV drama "W.I.O.U.," Hartley's intensely
personal memoirs, "Breaking the Silence," were published by
Putnam Books in October of this year. Publishers Weekly says of
the tell-all tome, "Sometimes hilarious, sometimes horrifying,
this splendid autobiography...rises well above other efforts of
its kind."

Without question, Mariette Hartley has become one of today's most
important actresses and humanitarians. From her acclaimed work
on stage with such notables as Hume Cronyn and Jessica Tandy to
her six Emmy nominations (and one Emmy win) for a diversity of
portrayals for television, Hartley has earned her stature as one
one of the entertainment industry's great ladies. Her tireless
efforts in helping humanity through myriad charitable
involvements has distinguished her career from its early
beginnings.

I hope the enclosed materials will inspire your interest in this
very talented and special lady. I look forward to discussing
your interest in Mariette.

Best regards,

Paul A. Baker

encl

153

9348 Civic Center Drive, Fourth Floor • Beverly Hills, California 90210 • (213) 278-1460 • Fax: (213) 278-2571
145 Avenue of the Americas, Second Floor • New York, NY 10013 • (212) 206-7160 • Fax: (212) 627-8733

9

CREDITS

Credits mean different things to different people. If you talk to an actor, they mean the shows he's done and the parts he's played. If you're talking to a producer, director, or writer, credits mean the shows they've produced, directed, or written.

If you're talking about a show, credits mean the names and information appearing on the opening titles and on the end crawl.

In this chapter, we are talking about show credits. Here, as elsewhere, we will see that there are different ways of handling these in press kits and press materials and the publicist should be guided by the policy of the company he or she is working for.

Reviewers for trade publications (*The Hollywood Reporter, Daily Variety*) usually want full credits. If the press kit only carries partial credits, the publicist must then provide the reviewer with a separate copy of the full credits (a Xeroxed copy of the credits obtained from the production company is fine). Please turn to Chapter 10 (Film Publicity Writing) to see what full credits look like (TV credits would be similar).

When dealing with credits, it's important to work from accurate information. That's why it's best to make contact with the person in the production company who will be responsible for putting the credits together. It is always best to work from copy. That lessens the chances of error. Otherwise, if you take information down over the phone, or in a meeting, you may forget to ask whether Carol is spelled with or without an "e," whether Cathy is with a "C" or a "K," or whether Sylbert is spelled with an "i" or a "y," not to mention even more unusual names which can get misspelled so easily.

Motion picture press kits tend to carry the full credits just as they are seen on the motion picture screen. Some TV press kits will do the same, especially when it comes to TV movies or miniseries.

But most TV press kits and releases use partial credits, plus such additional information as the show's format, date, time, and place of broadcast. Whether you use full credits or selective credits, it is absolutely important that you are accurate not only in the way you spell a person's name but in the way you list that person's category. "Starring" is different from "co-starring" which is different from "also starring." A "special guest star" is different from a "guest star." "Featuring" is different from "with" which is different from "introducing."

An "executive producer" is different from a "producer" who is different from an "associate producer" or a "co-producer" or an "executive in charge of production." "Teleplay by" is different from "story by." And writer credits of "Joe Doe and Jane Doe" mean something different from "Joe Doe & Jane Doe" (an "and" and an "ampersand" have different legal meanings).

You will also want to follow the order in which credits appear on the screen, since the billing order represents the relative importance of the talent and production staff.

So, to the question, "What's in a name?" the answer is, "A lot." As for the question, "What's in a title?" the answer is, "Careers!"

Credits are contractual matters. There are legal issues involved. Don't treat credits casually. When in doubt, check it out.

CREDITS FOR 'CHEERS'

Time:	NBC Television Network broadcasts <u>Thursdays</u> (9–9:30 p.m. NYT)
Premiere:	September 29, 1982
Format:	Comedy series about the camaraderie and lively debates in a cozy, sports–oriented Boston bar, and the relationship between the street–wise ex–ballplayer bartender, Sam Malone, his boss, Rebecca Howe, the staff and the colorful parade of customers who frequent the bar.
Starring	Ted Danson as Sam Malone
Co–starring	Rhea Perlman as Carla Tortelli; George Wendt as Norm Peterson; John Ratzenberger as Cliff Clavin; Woody Harrelson as Woody Boyd; Kelsey Grammer as Frasier Crane; and Kirstie Alley as Rebecca Howe
Executive producers:	James Burrows, Glen Charles, Les Charles
Created by	Glen Charles & Les Charles and James Burrows
Directed by	James Burrows
Producers:	Peter Casey, David Lee and David Angell
Executive script consultant:	David Lloyd
Executive in charge of production:	Richard Villarino
Co–producer:	Tim Berry
Director of photography:	John Finger
Original set design by	Richard Sylbert
Production:	Charles/Burrows/Charles Productions in association with Paramount Television
Origination:	Paramount Studios, Los Angeles, CA
NBC Media Relations rep.:	Mark J. Kern, 818/840–4630

————o————   Fall, 1987

156

CREDITS FOR NBC-TV'S 'THE SUN ALSO RISES'

Time:	NBC Television Network colorcasts, Sunday, December 9 (9-11 p.m. NYT) and Monday, December 10 (9-11 p.m. NYT).
Format:	Dramatic four-hour NBC-TV miniseries based on the classic Hemingway novel about American expatriates trying to find themselves in Europe just after World War I.
Starring:	Jane Seymour as Lady Brett Ashley Hart Bochner as Jake Barnes Leonard Nimoy as The Count Ian Charleson as Mike Campbell Robert Carradine as Robert Cohn Zeljko Ivanek as Bill Gorton Stephane Audran as Georgette Andrea Occhipinti as Pedro
Executive Producer:	John Furia, Jr.
Producer/Writer:	Robert L. Joseph
Director:	James Goldstone
Associate Producer:	Jean Pierre Avice
Director of Photography:	Jacques Robin
Production Designer:	Francois de Lamothe
Art Directors:	Jacques Brizzio and Jose Maria Tapiador
Film Editors:	Richard E. Rabjohn and Robert P. Seppey
Sound Mixer:	Colin Charles
Music:	Billy Goldenberg
Costume Designer:	Catherine Gorne
Jane Seymour's wardrobe by:	Chanel
Make-up:	Antoine Garabedian
Originiation:	Filmed on location in France and Spain
Produced by:	20th Century Fox Television
NBC Press Representative:	Barry Cherin (Burbank)

——o——

November, 1984
#1188Y

157

SARAH, PLAIN AND TALL

CAST AND CREDITS

Following are the cast and production credits for the HALLMARK HALL OF FAME presentation of "Sarah, Plain and Tall," based on the Newbery Medal-winning children's book by Patricia MacLachlan.

Attracted by a newspaper advertisement, Sarah (Glenn Close) leaves the serenity and security of her seacoast home in Maine and travels to the Kansas prairie, where she enters the lives of two motherless children and their stern and lonely father, Jacob (Christopher Walken).

PROGRAM:	"Sarah, Plain and Tall"
SERIES:	HALLMARK HALL OF FAME
AIRDATE AND TIME:	Sunday, February 3, 1991 at 9 p.m. ET on CBS
STORY LINE:	The trials and tribulations of turn-of-the-century life on the Kansas prairie are felt vividly as Sarah Wheaton attempts to fill the void in the lives of two children and their widowed father.
EXECUTIVE PRODUCERS:	William Self Glenn Close
PRODUCED AND DIRECTED BY:	Glenn Jordan
SUPERVISING PRODUCER:	Edwin Self
TELEPLAY BY:	Patricia MacLachlan Carol Sobieski

Hallmark
Hall of Fame
158

BASED ON THE BOOK BY: Patricia MacLachlan

MUSIC BY: David Shire

EDITED BY: John Wright

PRODUCTION DESIGNER: Ed Wittstein

DIRECTOR OF PHOTOGRAPHY: Michael Fash

COSTUME DESIGNER: Van Broughton Ramsey

STARRING: Glenn Close
                         Christopher Walken
                         Lexi Randall
                         Margaret Sophie Stein
                         Jon De Vries

INTRODUCING: Christopher Bell

"Sarah, Plain and Tall," the 168th HALLMARK HALL OF FAME presentation, is from Self Productions, Inc. and Trillium Productions, Inc. It was filmed entirely on location in Kansas, Nebraska and Maine.

# # #

Press Contacts:

Stone/Hallinan Associates, Inc.   Hallmark Cards, Inc.
Los Angeles: 213/655-8970   Television Programming
New York: 212/489-5590   816/274-8099

7449 MELROSE AVENUE. LOS ANGELES. CA 90046 (213) 655-8970   1350 AVENUE OF THE AMERICAS. NEW YORK. NY 10019 (212) 489-5590

CBS MEDIA RELATIONS
51 WEST 52 STREET
NEW YORK, NY 10019

November 19, 1990

Following are cast and production credits for DONOR, a new motion picture-for-television to be broadcast on the "CBS Sunday Movie," Sunday, Dec. 9 on the CBS Television Network:

ON AIR:	9:00-11:00 PM, ET/PT
FORMAT:	Thriller about a young female doctor who stumbles across a series of mysterious events at a hospital, including human experimentation, murder and a horrifying coverup
ORIGINATION:	Filmed on location in Los Angeles
STARRING:	Melissa Gilbert-Brinkman (Dr. Kristine Lipton) Jack Scalia (Dr. Eugene Kesselman) Wendy Hughes (Dr. Farrell) Gregory Sierra (Hector Aliosa) Gale Mayron (Melody) Marc Lawrence (Ben Beliot)
AND:	Pernell Roberts as Dr. Martingale
PRODUCED BY:	CBS Entertainment Productions in association with Peter Frankovich/ Daniel A. Sherkow Productions
EXECUTIVE PRODUCERS:	Daniel A. Sherkow Peter Frankovich
PRODUCER:	Ken Swor
WRITTEN BY:	Michael Braverman
DIRECTED BY:	Larry Shaw
CO-STARRING:	Wendy Cooke as Robby Elias Michael Boatman (Arnold) Hari Rhodes (Harry) Carol Ann Susi (Berlinetti)
MUSIC BY:	Gary Chang
EDITED BY:	Mark Westmore
PRODUCTION DESIGNER:	Peter Wooley

(More)

DIRECTOR OF PHOTOGRAPHY:	Neil Roach
FEATURING:	Virginia Capers (Mrs. Mantley)
	Larry Cedar (Roger Ebersole)
	Don Alan Croll (Rabbi)
	David Crowley (Dr. Marjorian)
	Gregory Daven (Harlan Barker)
	Ruth Ekholm (Nurse)
	Gail Fisher (Secretary)
	Pedro Gonzalez-Gonzalez (Hispanic Man)
	Robert Kim (Surgical Resident)
	Emily Kuroda (ICU Nurse)
	Toni Lawrence (Dr. Karen Steinbrook)
	Michael Matthews (Willy)
	Dorothy Neumann (Elderly Woman)
	Liana Odalys (Duty Nurse)
	Jeff Olan (Anesthetist)
	Al Scheckwitz (Crater)
	Sunni Walton (M/S Patient)
PRODUCTION MIXER:	Bill Teague
SOUND EDITOR:	Joseph Melody
EXECUTIVE IN CHARGE OF PRODUCTION:	Norman S. Powell
PRESS REPRESENTATIVES:	Elaine Mallon (Los Angeles)
	Hali Simon (New York)

. . .

10

FILM PUBLICITY WRITING

The raw material with which television publicists and motion picture publicists work is the same in most respects. Much of what I have said in this book about television publicity writing applies to motion picture publicity writing.

However, there are some differences which are important to keep in mind. There are some structural differences between television press kits and motion picture press kits, for instance.

If you look at Warner Bros.' "Driving Miss Daisy" press kit in this chapter, you will see how items are used as production notes and how these are written differently from television items (as discussed in chapter 6). You will see how some information which is handled separately in television releases is combined under an umbrella heading in motion picture publicity. Storylines and biographies become part of the "Production Information" section ("About the Cast...," "About the Filmmakers..."), where all this material is presented in continuous order.

A separate book could and may be written on publicity writing for motion pictures. However, much can be learned by doing what I have suggested all along -- study a good example of a news release or press kit, particularly the one that you are expected to follow. The "Driving Miss Daisy" press kit is a good example of a motion picture press kit. However, it is no more representative of *all* motion picture press kits than any one television press kit is representative of *all* television press kits. Motion picture press kits vary in style the way television press kits vary in style, as you go from studio to studio, agency to agency, production company to production company. However, all motion picture press kits share certain major elements in common. This is certainly an excellent press kit and provides a good example of those elements.

Motion picture publicity writing also differs from television publicity writing because of the different time schedule involved in the making of a motion picture.

I highly recommend a book, *REEL EXPOSURE: How to Publicize and Promote Today's Motion Pictures* (Broadway Press, Shelter Island, NY 1991), by veteran Hollywood film publicist Steven Jay Rubin. It is the definitive primer on every aspect of motion picture publicity. It could have been subtitled "Everything You Ever Wanted to Know about Motion Picture Publicity But Were Afraid to Ask." If you are into underlining important information, prepare to underline just about every word of every sentence of every paragraph of every page. Do I exaggerate? No. I have *understated* the case! This book is valuable to every individual -- from the person wishing to enter this field to the veteran publicist. It should be in every entertainment PR office. You can conduct a successful PR campaign, from beginning to end, just following this book by the numbers. *REEL EXPOSURE* also contains some good advice about motion picture publicity writing, including several examples. The book is available at such Hollywood book stores as Larry Edmunds, Samuel French and Book Soup. For additional information you may contact the publisher toll free at 1-800-869-6372.

Following is a list of what a motion picture publicist needs to know how to write:

PRE-PRODUCTION

Casting news
Staff news
Trade items
Announcement story

PRODUCTION
Start of production story
Positioning statement
Biographies
Advance production notes
Pitch letter
Colum items
Memos
       Production publicity outline
       Progress reports
       Wrap-up memo
Press kit (final)
Photo captions
End of production story

POST-PRODUCTION
If there was no production PR
coverage, much of the above
material must be generated now
and/or during the pre-release
period

PRE-RELEASE PERIOD
Strategy letter
Invitations (to screenings)
One-sheets
Pitch letters
Progress reports

"DRIVING MISS DAISY"

- Production Information -

Miss Daisy Werthan (JESSICA TANDY), a highly independent, eccentric 72-year-old Southern Jewish matron, manages to crash her new 1948 Packard directly into her neighbor's garden. Daisy is unscathed by the accident, but her son Boolie (DAN AYKROYD), fearing for her future safety, urges his reluctant mother to hire a chauffeur. Daisy bitterly resents the notion that she is anything but completely capable of taking care of herself.

Without Daisy's consent, Boolie hires a driver, Hoke Colburn (MORGAN FREEMAN)--a stalwart and very patient black widower in his early 60s. Finally resigned to Boolie's plan, Daisy agrees to the idea of having someone else drive her, thus beginning a friendship that will abide for the next 25 years, echoing decades of social change. Daisy and Hoke become a beguiling "odd couple," their friendship ultimately testing the limits of their differences...and similarities.

Set against the backdrop of the changing American South, The Zanuck Company's "Driving Miss Daisy," released by Warner Bros., interweaves the touching and humorous stories of its central characters--Miss Daisy, Hoke, Boolie, his social-climbing wife Florine (PATTI LuPONE) and Miss Daisy's longtime housekeeper Idella (ESTHER ROLLE).

The screen adaptation of ALFRED UHRY's Pulitzer Prize-winning play is produced by RICHARD D. ZANUCK ("Jaws,"

"The Sting," "The Verdict," "Cocoon," "Cocoon: The Return")
and LILI FINI ZANUCK ("Cocoon," "Cocoon: The Return"). The
film is directed by BRUCE BERESFORD, an Academy Award nominee
for "Tender Mercies" whose other credits include "Breaker
Morant" and "Crimes of the Heart." Mr. Uhry adapted his own
play for the screen.

Lending their behind-the-camera talents to "Driving
Miss Daisy" are director of photography PETER JAMES, pro-
duction designer BRUNO RUBEO ("Platoon"), costume designer
ELIZABETH McBRIDE ("Tender Mercies"), composer HANS ZIMMER
(an Oscar nominee for "Rain Man") and editor MARK WARNER
("A Soldier's Story").

About the Production...

How is a Pulitzer Prize-winning play born? For Alfred
Uhry, it began when he was asked by New York stage producers
Jane Harmon and Nina Keneally to critique another play they
were considering. After reading the manuscript, Uhry's only
comment was "That's not reality"...and then set out to write
a play about "real people."

What emerged was "Driving Miss Daisy," loosely based on
the experiences of Uhry's grandmother, Lena Fox, and her
chauffeur, Will Coleman. Says the writer, "It's my grandmother,
it's her sisters, it's my mother, it's me in a bad mood, it's
my wife when she's feisty, it's probably what I happened to
eat for breakfast that day. It's all of that."

-more-

More seriously, the story was intended to serve as a metaphor of the relationship between Southern white and black cultures in the period of the emerging Civil Rights movement--but crystallized in the story of the characters created by Uhry. "It interested me to write about two minority figures," says the writer, "one of whom was able to come to terms with being a victim of prejudice, and one who wasn't."

The story blends with actual events in Atlanta's history, including the 1958 bombing of The Temple--the city's oldest Jewish congregation--and later in the story, the ceremony in January 1965 at the Dinkler Plaza Hotel, where the Reverend Dr. Martin Luther King, Jr. was honored.

According to stage producer Harmon, "there was a magic to the story" from the outset. Under the aegis of Playwrights Horizons, the play opened in 1985 at the company's 74-seat Studio Theatre. The initial five week run was extended, and the incredible demand that developed necessitated a move to a larger theatre down the street--where, remarkably, "Driving Miss Daisy" still continues four years later.

"Driving Miss Daisy" went on to win several Obie Awards--including one for Morgan Freeman, who created the role of Hoke--and ultimately the Pulitzer Prize for Uhry. In subsequent months, productions were established in Chicago, Los Angeles, Toronto and Atlanta, with additional companies touring the country. International productions opened in London, Vienna, Norway, the Soviet Union and other

-more-

far-flung corners of the globe.

That "Driving Miss Daisy" would find its way to the screen seemed inevitable in light of its extraordinary theatrical success. Shortly after the play opened in New York City, it came to the attention of producers Richard and Lili Zanuck, who wasted no time in scooping up the motion picture rights.

The first order of business was to develop the screen-play, and the Zanucks immediately turned to Alfred Uhry (who at that time, in addition to the continuing success of "Driving Miss Daisy," was also enjoying rave reviews for "Mystic Pizza," his first filmed script).

The Zanucks were determined that while the scope of the play needed to be expanded for the screen, no sacri-fices would be made in the uncompromising quality of the original. "We worked with Alfred to open up the story," says Lili Zanuck, "but the worst thing you can do is to try to manufacture a hit. We set out to live up to the integrity of the play."

Uhry also needed to make the movie work on its own terms. "'Miss Daisy' was so ingrained in my mind as a play," admits Uhry, "and the original line readings were always in my ears. I finally had to ask myself objectively, if I were going to see a movie of this play...what would I want to see?"

Upon the playwright's completion of the screenplay, the Zanucks approached Australian-born, Oscar-nominated

-more-

filmmaker Bruce Beresford to direct. "We greatly admired Bruce's fresh viewpoint of the American South in 'Tender Mercies' and 'Crimes of the Heart,'" says Richard Zanuck. "We felt he would bring a perspective to the story that we wouldn't necessarily find with someone else." Beresford responded immediately to the project.

"I don't know why I've done so many Southern stories," comments the director. "Horton Foote, Beth Henley and Alfred Uhry all wrote stories that were primarily autobiographical with a great deal of simplicity and directness. Those are the kinds of stories I like to film, and perhaps it's just coincidence that they all happen to be Southern."

Casting became a particular joy for the filmmakers. "There's nothing more satisfying than making a movie with the people who you really believe should be in it," explains Lili Zanuck.

In what was to become a greatly sought-after role, the Zanucks and Beresford chose Jessica Tandy to play Miss Daisy. "Some very important actresses were suggested to us," recalls Richard Zanuck, "most of them stars in their 30s and 40s. But very early on we came to the conclusion that it would be a catastrophic mistake to 'age' somebody. After all, in the story Daisy begins at age 70." Lili Zanuck elaborates, "The idea of spending hours and hours applying prosthetics to a young woman would be an awful thing to do. It's also a form of discrimination of the

-more-

worst type--when there are wonderful actors of the appropriate age, why not cast them? That's the philosophy we
stood by with 'Cocoon,' and the results more than proved
we were right."

    Alfred Uhry is even more pointed. "There are," he
says simply, "no better actresses alive than Jessica Tandy.
She's a national treasure."

    Miss Tandy herself was excited about the challenge of
making Miss Daisy come fully alive on screen. "It's a wonderful script and a wonderful part," she notes enthusiasti-
cally. "And although the relationship is a universal one,
it has particular significance in its Southern milieu."

    To play Hoke, Morgan Freeman--who created the role
off-Broadway--was everyone's first choice. "Morgan brings
a dimension to this part that from the beginning has to do
with things that I couldn't write and can barely explain,"
notes Uhry. "It's a combination of irony, dignity and
humility that's quite indefinable."

    "Some parts reach out and grab you," muses Freeman,
"and no matter what, you have to do them. You settle into
them like old shoes...Hoke was one of those roles. I was
floored when I first read the play. I just knew Hoke so
intimately. I suppose it has to do with my background,
and the South, and my deep and abiding appreciation for
those kinds of people--the Hokes, the Idellas, the Daisys--
who they were, how they lived and why."

    For the role of Boolie, Miss Daisy's exasperated but

-more-

loyal businessman son, the filmmakers chose Dan Aykroyd, one
of America's favorite actors. Recalls Aykroyd, "A friend
of mine had seen the play and suggested that I should do the
movie. I found out who was doing it and met with Bruce
Beresford, who handed me the script. I read it cold, which
I haven't done since 1970. But I had nothing to lose."

Aykroyd's reading for Beresford turned out to be a
resounding success, and the actor was immediately enlisted
for the production.

Completing the versatile cast are Patti LuPone as
Florine and Esther Rolle as Idella, both immediate consensus
choices with their tremendous backgrounds on stage, screen
and television.

In bringing Uhry's play to cinematic reality, the
filmmakers faced the challenge of recreating 25 years of
Atlanta history on a relatively spartan budget. Production
designer Bruno Rubeo was charged with the considerable task
of turning back the clock to 1948, and then forward again
through the years to 1973.

While few existing locations in Atlanta resemble the
city of the 1940s and '50s, they were fortunate to discover
a neighborhood in the verdant Druid Hills section that
looks almost completely untouched. Coincidentally, the
company chose a lovely red brick house--surrounded by
dogwoods and magnolias--for the principal location of
Miss Daisy's home. It was a house, unknown to the

-more-

filmmakers when conducting their search, that was previously owned by a "Southern cousin" of Alfred Uhry, and one that the writer played in as a child.

For the film's early scenes, Euclid Avenue--in the bohemian Atlanta neighborhood known as "Little Five Points"--brought forth unusual feelings of deja vu for Atlantans old enough to remember what their city looked like in 1948. The Sevananda Natural Foods Cooperative-- a vegetarian supermarket--was converted into the Piggly Wiggly, with an impressive period sign, a black-and-white awning and prices posted that looked like a budgeter's dream: a quarter for a quart of milk, four cans of peas for 42 cents and 10 pounds of sugar for 72 cents. A vintage Coca-Cola advertisement took up an entire side wall of the Piggly Wiggly, with the Sevananda's usual customers shaking their heads in disbelief.

Nearby, the African Connections store was converted into the Southern Stamp and Stencil Co.; the Ellis Theatre was magically reinvented as the Variety Theatre (with the marquee announcing the engagement of "Gentleman's Agreement," a classic 1947 film about social intolerance); and various other accoutrements of the day, including telephone booths, a men's clothing store featuring suits with very wide lapels and motor vehicles caught in the glorious time warp created by Rubeo and his crew.

Griffin, a small town 45 miles from Atlanta that

-more-

171

closely resembled the city as it used to be, doubled for
some exterior shots, and a downtown Atlanta supply company
was transformed into the elaborate cotton mill owned by
Boolie Werthan.

Making certain that the costumes fit both the period
and the actors was designer Elizabeth McBride, who had
previously collaborated with Bruce Beresford on "Tender
Mercies" and provided a more comic look at middle American
styles in David Byrne's "True Stories." Having been born
and raised in Shreveport, Louisiana, McBride was certainly
familiar with "Driving Miss Daisy"'s milieu.

"I'm from the South," she explains, "and when I was
a child I was surrounded by characters like Daisy, Hoke,
Boolie, Florine and the others. Many of my ideas for their
costumes came from my own memories."

McBride's costumes for "Driving Miss Daisy" are a
combination of "built" costumes (those designed by her and
newly made) and actual clothing from the periods covered in
the film. "At the time we shot the movie," McBride recalls,
"there were several other period films being made at the
same time. The racks were empty in Hollywood's major
costume houses, so my team and I had to shop in Atlanta,
San Francisco and Dallas and buy what we needed."

As clothes and setting often help to define characters, McBride worked very closely with Beresford, Rubeo
and the actors to make sure that everyone was outfitted

-more-

properly. "As a wealthy Southern matron, Miss Daisy dresses with care and style, but often wears the same dresses for years," notes McBride. "Florine, on the other hand, is a classic nouveau riche wife, and has to wear whatever is most popular at that particular moment. She's much more flamboyant than Daisy."

Assembling the vintage cars required to illustrate 25 years of driving was the job of transportation captain J.L. Parker and car wrangler Ray Suttles, who brought together more than 350 cars and trucks, after conducting a national car search. For Miss Daisy's cars, countless automobiles were "auditioned," but most didn't meet the particular requirements of having four doors (appropriate for chauffeur and passenger) or were not the dark colors suited to Miss Daisy's conservative taste. Compounding the situation was the job of finding "matching" cars for the elaborate camera work.

And what were some of the good citizens of Atlanta doing during the location filming of "Driving Miss Daisy"? Watching, of course. Whether familiar with the play, Atlantans--both black and white--expressed great interest not only in the behind-the-scenes details of shooting a major feature film, but in the story of Daisy and Hoke as well.

"It's our story too, isn't it?," noted one by-stander on Euclid Avenue. "All of our stories. A lot has changed in this city over the last 40 years or so...be-

-more-

cause a lot has changed inside of the people who live here."

Warner Bros. presents A Zanuck Company Production, Morgan Freeman, Jessica Tandy and Dan Aykroyd starring in "Driving Miss Daisy." The motion picture also stars Patti Lupone and Esther Rolle. "Driving Miss Daisy" is directed by Bruce Beresford and produced by Richard D. Zanuck and Lili Fini Zanuck. The screenplay is by Alfred Uhry, based on his play. David Brown is the executive producer. The music for the film is composed by Hans Zimmer. Peter James, A.C.S. is the director of photography, Bruno Rubeo is the production designer and Mark Warner is the editor. The co-executive producer is Jake Eberts.

About the Cast...

MORGAN FREEMAN (Hoke Colburn) is one of the stage and screen's most versatile and distinguished actors. His recent triumphs include two Warner Bros. films--as the tough drug rehabilitation counselor in "Clean and Sober," and as controversial high-school principal Joe Clark in "Lean On Me."

Freeman came to national prominence when he was nominated for both an Academy Award and a Golden Globe Award for his electrifying supporting performance in 1987's "Street Smart," which also brought him honors from the New York, Los Angeles and National Society of Film Critics. In her review of the film, The New Yorker's Pauline Kael asked, "Is Morgan Freeman the greatest American actor?"...and then went on to answer her own query in the affirmative.

-more-

Making his off-Broadway debut in 1967 with "The Niggerlovers," Freeman followed quickly with his Broadway debut in "Hello, Dolly!," with Pearl Bailey and Cab Calloway, and he subsequently took over the title role in the musical "Purlie!" He received a Drama Desk Award, Clarence Derwent Award and was nominated for a Tony Award for his Broadway performance in "The Mighty Gents," and has been the recipient of three Obie Awards--the first for the title role of "Coriolanus" at the New York Shakespeare Festival and the second for the lead of "The Gospel at Colonus," which he repeated in the acclaimed 1988 Broadway production.

Freeman won his third Obie when he created the role of Hoke Colburn in the original off-Broadway production of "Driving Miss Daisy."

He recently completed roles in the theatrical features "Johnny Handsome" and "Glory."

With a professional career that has spanned 64 years, JESSICA TANDY (Daisy Werthan) is one of the first ladies of the American theatre.

Born in London, England, she made her stage debut at age 16 and was performing on the New York stage when she was 21. A winner of three Tony Awards, Tandy received the first for creating the role of Blanche DuBois in the Tennessee Williams classic "A Streetcar Named Desire," and won two more for her performances with husband Hume Cronyn in "The Gin Game" and "Foxfire."

Miss Tandy's motion picture debut was in the 1932

-more-

175

production of "The Indiscretion of Eve." Since then she has appeared in such films as "The Seventh Cross," "The Green Years," "Dragonwyck," "Forever Amber," "September Affair," "The Desert Fox," "The Light in the Forest," "Hemingway's Adventures of a Young Man," "The Birds," "Honky Tonk Freeway," "Best Friends," "The Bostonians," "*batteries not included," "Cocoon" and "Cocoon: The Return," which marked her sixth film appearance with Hume Cronyn.

In 1986, Miss Tandy and Cronyn were recognized for their outstanding contributions to the arts at the Kennedy Center Honors in Washington, D.C. Miss Tandy's numerous other honors include the Delia Austrian Medal for "Five Finger Exercise," the Obie and Drama Desk Awards for "Not I," the Sarah Siddons Award for "The Gin Game" and the Emmy Award as Best Actress for the Hallmark Hall of Fame production of "Foxfire."

DAN AYKROYD (Boolie Werthan), one of America's favorite actors, has delighted audiences worldwide with his mercurial and hilarious characterizations in a series of wildly successful films.

Catapulting to stardom with a five-year stint on "Saturday Night Live," the Canadian-born actor earned an Emmy Award in 1977. With fellow "Blues Brother" John Belushi, Aykroyd was one of the first "SNL" players to find success on the big screen. He and Belushi became a dynamic theatrical team that starred in "The Blues Brothers" (which Aykroyd originated and co-wrote), "1941" and "Neighbors."

Aykroyd's other screen credits includ "Trading Places"

-more-

with "Saturday Night Live" alumnus Eddie Murphy, "Doctor
Detroit," "Spies Like Us" (which he also originated and co-
wrote), the blockbuster "Ghostbusters" (originated, co-
wrote), "Dragnet" (also co-wrote), "The Couch Trip," "The
Great Outdoors," "My Stepmother Is An Alien" and
"Ghostbusters II" (originated, co-wrote).

Aykroyd made cameo appearances in "Twilight Zone -
The Movie" and "Into the Night" and produced the feature
"One More Saturday Night" for tape and cable markets.

PATTI LuPONE (Florine) is perhaps best remembered for
her stunning Tony and Drama Desk Award winning portrayal
of the title role in the Broadway musical "Evita." She is
currently starring on the acclaimed new ABC-TV series
"Life Goes On."

A graduate of the Juilliard School, and a founding
member of The Acting Company, LuPone first worked with
"Driving Miss Daisy" writer Alfred Uhry on "The Robber
Bridegroom," for which she received a Tony nomination. She
has worked extensively on and off-Broadway, as well as in
London with the Royal Shakespeare Company.

"Driving Miss Daisy" re-unites LuPone with Dan Aykroyd,
with whom she first worked in Steven Spielberg's "1941." Her
other feature film credits include "Wise Guys" and "Witness."
She also received national attention for her performance as
Lady Bird Johnson in NBC's "LBJ: The Early Years."

ESTHER ROLLE (Idella) starred for five years on NBC's
popular situation comedy "Good Times," but like her "Driving

-more-

Miss Daisy" colleagues Morgan Freeman, Jessica Tandy and Patti LuPone, she has a greatly accomplished New York theatre background.

As the ninth of 18 children, Rolle formed a musical dramatic group with her siblings and performed for local functions. The journalism career she had planned while attending Atlanta's Spellman College turned into a passion for theatre. She moved to New York City, attended the New York School for Social Research, and helped make history as one of the original members of the famed Negro Ensemble Company.

Rolle's talents soon found a niche on Broadway, where her credits include "Don't Play Us Cheap" and two James Baldwin plays, "Amen Corner" and "Blues for Mr. Charlie." Off-Broadway she appeared in "Black Girl" and Jean Genet's "The Blacks." More recently, she received rave reviews while starring in the Broadway revival of Carson McCullers' "A Member of the Wedding."

Aside from her stint on "Good Times," Rolle garnered attention for the recent PBS production of Lorraine Hansberry's "A Raisin in the Sun." She won an Emmy for her stellar performance in the NBC television movie "The Summer of My Summer Soldier," starred in Maya Angelou's "I Know Why the Caged Bird Sings" and portrayed pioneer Mary Fields in the award-winning PBS series, "South By Northwest."

-more-

About the Filmmakers...

One of the top producers in Hollywood, RICHARD D. ZANUCK has always been a leader in the film industry. He spent much of his youth learning all aspects of film production at Twentieth Century Fox during the 30-year-reign of his legendary father, Darryl F. Zanuck. Upon graduation from Stanford University and a stint as an Army lieutenant, Zanuck joined his father as a story and production assistant on two Fox films, "Island in the Sun" and "The Sun Also Rises."

Zanuck made his debut as a full-fledged producer at the age of 24 with the feature "Compulsion," winner of three awards at the Cannes Film Festival. He followed it in 1961 with "Sanctuary," based on the William Faulkner novel, and in 1962 with "The Chapman Report." At the age of 34, he was named president of Twentieth Century Fox.

During his eight years at the helm of Fox, the studio returned to the greatness of its heyday. Under his aegis, the studio's films received 159 Oscar nominations, and won Best Picture Academy Awards for "The Sound of Music," "Patton" and "The French Connection."

In 1972, Zanuck and long-time associate David Brown formed The Zanuck/Brown Company, one of the motion picture industry's most distinguished and successful independent production entities. The Zanuck/Brown Company was responsible for such major box office blockbusters as "Jaws," "Jaws 2," "The Sting," "The Verdict" and "Cocoon."

-more-

"Driving Miss Daisy" is the inaugural production of the recently established The Zanuck Company.

LILI FINI ZANUCK (Producer) made her debut as a producer on "Cocoon," shepherding the Academy Award-winning film from its initial development to critical acclaim and commercial success. Given the responsibility of finding and developing new talent for The Zanuck/Brown Company, she came across the unpublished manuscript of David Saperstein's novel and developed it into screenplay form. For her work she was named, with Richard D. Zanuck and David Brown, Producer of the Year in 1985 by the National Association of Theatre Owners (NATO).

Previously, Zanuck served as a research assistant at the World Bank in Washington, D.C. and in office management with The Carnation Company in Los Angeles.

Prior to "Cocoon," Zanuck helped develop "The Island," "Neighbors" and "The Verdict" at The Zanuck/Brown Company, and she also produced "Cocoon: The Return" with Richard D. Zanuck.

BRUCE BERESFORD (Director) won a 1980 Academy Award nomination for co-writing the screenplay for "Breaker Morant" and received another Oscar nomination in 1984 for directing "Tender Mercies."

Born and raised in Australia, Beresford attended the University of Sydney and worked in advertising and tele-vision until he travelled to England in 1961, where he did various jobs while trying to break into the film industry.

-more-

In 1964, he took a job as a film editor in Nigeria, which lasted two years. Upon his return to England, he was appointed head of the British Film Institute Production Board but returned to Australia in the early '70s determined to make his own films.

"Don's Party" and "The Getting of Wisdom" established him as one of Australia's premier directors. But it was "Breaker Morant" that confirmed his outstanding talents, becoming a worldwide hit and garnering international acclaim. The film won 11 Australian Film Institute Awards.

Before making his American motion picture debut with "Tender Mercies," Beresford directed two other Australian films, "The Club" and "Puberty Blues." His other film credits are "King David," "The Fringe Dwellers," "Crimes of the Heart" and "Her Alibi." Beresford also directed a segment of the 1988 film "Aria," which highlighted Erich Wolfgang Korngold's music from "Die Totestadt."

ALFRED UHRY (Writer/Associate Producer) won the coveted Pulitzer Prize for "Driving Miss Daisy," one of the most acclaimed plays in years.

Born and raised in Atlanta, Georgia, Uhry moved to New York City after graduating from Brown University in 1958. He formed a partnership with Bob Waldman, and worked for famed composer Frank Loesser as a songwriter for ads and television.

In 1975, Uhry wrote the book for the Broadway musical "The Robber Bridegroom," and was honored with a Tony

-more-

nomination and two Drama Desk Awards for his efforts. He also wrote the musical "Chapeau" for John Houseman's Acting Company. After writing the lyrics for "Swing," Uhry reconstructed five old musical comedy librettos for the Goodspeed over the next four years. His last musical was "America's Sweetheart" (1984-85).

Uhry's prior screen credit was the hit "Mystic Pizza." He is currently at work on another play, also set in Atlanta and based on his youth, as well as a number of screen projects.

"Driving Miss Daisy" will mark the American feature debut for Australian PETER JAMES (Director of Photography). He was awarded the Best Cinematography prize from the Australian Film Institute in 1985 for Michael Jenkins' "Rebel" and in 1986 for Di Drew's "The Right Hand Man." He was also awarded the Australian Cinematographer of the Year Award in 1976 for Donald Crombie's "Caddie," and in 1971 for Greg Ropert's "Willy Willy."

James' work was seen in the United States earlier this year in Phillip Noyce's "Echoes of Paradise," filmed in Thailand.

After attending film school in Rome, Italy, BRUNO RUBEO (Production Designer) started his professional career working with special effects wizard Carlo Rambaldi ("E.T. the Extra-Terrestrial," "Alien"). In 1968, Rubeo moved to New York City, where he worked in advertising for five years. After moving to Toronto, he became art director for "City

-more-

TV," one of Canada's most innovative television stations.

In 1977, Rubeo moved to Los Angeles, rejoining Rambaldi and assisting on the design of a futuristic theme park--a project which was delayed when they both moved to Mexico City to work on the massive production of "Dune." Rubeo handled the movement of the special effects creatures for the David Lynch film.

Shortly thereafter, Rubeo met Oliver Stone, and has since served as production designer on the director's "Salvador," "Platoon," "Talk Radio" and the forthcoming "Born on the Fourth of July." His other production designer credits include "Walker," "Blood Red" and the recent epic "Old Gringo."

ELIZABETH McBRIDE (Costume Designer) grew up in Shreveport, Louisiana, and graduated from LSU with a degree in landscape architecture.

She started her professional career in Dallas in the late 1970s, and first worked with Bruce Beresford on "Tender Mercies." Her other features include David Byrne's "True Stories" and Daniel Petrie's "Square Dance." McBride also worked with Jessica Tandy and Hume Cronyn on the Emmy Award-winning Hallmark Hall of Fame production of "Foxfire."

HANS ZIMMER (Composer) was nominated for an Academy Award for the 1988 blockbuster "Rain Man." He also produced the music for "The Last Emperor," which was awarded Oscar and Grammy Awards for Best Original Score.

Zimmer has established himself as one of the most

-more-

innovative and sought-after composers in both the United States and England. He began his career in London as a jingle composer, and later co-wrote (with Stanley Myers) the scores for the features "Moonlighting," "Insignificance" and "Castaway." His individual efforts include "Burning Secret," "A World Apart," "Paperhouse" and "Wonderland."

Most recently, Zimmer has written the music for Ridley Scott's "Black Rain" and John Badham's upcoming "Bird on A Wire."

MARK WARNER (Editor) was born in Los Angeles and attended university in San Diego and San Francisco. He started working odd jobs in film while still in high school, learning the ropes in commercials and documentaries.

Deciding to become a film editor, he began assisting in that area in 1978. His break came when he was appointed a co-editor of "Rocky III" in 1982, followed by co-editing assignments on "48 HRS." and "Staying Alive." Warner became a full editor on Norman Jewison's "A Soldier's Story" in 1984 and has since served in the same capacity on "Weird Science," "Big Trouble in Little China," "The Running Man" and "Cocoon: The Return."

-wb-

EV.7

11/2/89

Photo Captions

WARNER BROS. Presents

A ZANUCK COMPANY Production

MORGAN FREEMAN

JESSICA TANDY

DAN AYKROYD

<u>DRIVING MISS DAISY</u>

PATTI LUPONE

ESTHER ROLLE

Directed by BRUCE BERESFORD

Produced by RICHARD D. ZANUCK and LILI FINI ZANUCK

Screenplay by ALFRED UHRY
Based on his play

Executive Producer DAVID BROWN

Director of Photography PETER JAMES, A.C.S.

Production Designer BRUNO RUBEO

Edited by MARK WARNER

Costume Designer ELIZABETH McBRIDE

Music Composed by HANS ZIMMER

186

THE CREDITS

Directed by	BRUCE BERESFORD
Produced by	RICHARD D. ZANUCK LILI FINI ZANUCK
Screenplay, based on his play, by	ALFRED UHRY
Executive Producer	DAVID BROWN
Director of Photography	PETER JAMES, A.C.S.
Production Designer	BRUNO RUBEO
Edited by	MARK WARNER
Costume Designer	ELIZABETH McBRIDE
Music Composed by	HANS ZIMMER
Co-Executive Producer	JAKE EBERTS
Associate Producers	ROBERT DOUDELL ALFRED UHRY
Unit Production Manager	ROBERT DOUDELL
1st Assistant Director	KATTERLI FRAUENFELDER
2nd Assistant Director	MARTHA ELCAN
Art Director	VICTOR KEMPSTER
Set Decorator	CRISPIAN SALLIS
Post Production Supervisor	RUSSELL PARIS
First Assistant Film Editor	STEVEN RAMIREZ
Assistant Film Editor	DONALD LIKOVICH
Apprentice Film Editor	JEREMIAH O'DRISCOLL
Music Editor	LAURA PERLMAN
Music Scoring Mixer	JAY RIFKIN
Music Supervisor	BARRY LEVINE
Re-recording Mixers	MICHAEL MINKLER MATTHEW IADAROLA, C.A.S.

187

Recordist...MATTHEW PATTERSON

Camera Operator..ERICH ROLAND

First Assistant Camera....................................DAVID JOHN FREDERICK

Second Assistant Camera...................................DAVID MEISTRICH

Script Supervisor...ANNETTE HAYWOOD-CARTER

Production Mixer...HANK GARFIELD

Boom Operator..ANDY ROVINS

Cableperson/2nd Boom.......................................GLORIA COOPER

Property...PHILIP STEUER

Wardrobe Supervisor..MARSHA PERLOFF

Costumers...SUSAN E. MICKEY
                                                          KRISTINE KEARNEY

Makeup Supervisor...MANLIO ROCCHETTI

Assistant Makeup..LYNN BARBER

Makeup Consultant...KEVIN HANEY

Hair Stylists..PHIL LIDO
                                                          PHILLIP IVEY

Gaffer..KEITH SHERER

Best Boy..JEFF BECKER

Key Grip..ROBERT KEMPF

Best Boy/Grip...DAVID SINRICH

Dolly Grip...MICHAEL JOHN FEDACK

Special Effects Coordinator...............................BOB SHELLEY

Special Effects Assistant..................................B.J. SHELLEY

Production Coordinator....................................TERESA M. YARBROUGH

Assistant Production Coordinator.........................NANETTE GUIDEBECK

Production Secretary.................................CHARLENE MURRAY/ROSE

Production Accountants.................................ROBERT E. LEE
                                                 ERIC P. STECKLER
                                                 WENDY M. PRICE

Assistant to the Producers.............................JUDITH SCHEFKE

Location Manager.......................................ANDREW M. COMINS

Assistant Location Manager.............................ROBERT BALLENTINE

Public Relations.......................................RONNI CHASEN

Unit Publicist...ROBERT HOFFMAN

Still Photographer.....................................SAM YOUNG EMERSON

Casting (Atlanta)......................................ELYN S. WRIGHT

Researcher...KATHERINE SHAW

Property Assistants....................................WILLIAM ZULLO
                                                 VERA SMITH
                                                 BENJAMIN BERESFORD

Construction Coordinator...............................TONY KUPERSMITH

Construction Foreman...................................PAUL HUGGINS

Lead Person..KRIS McGARY

Head Set Dresser.......................................WREN BONEY

Set Dressers...KAREN YOUNG
                                                 JOHN OLIVEIRA
                                                 GARY L. BUCKLES

Scenic Chargeman.......................................DON E. COCHRAN

Transportation Coordinator.............................J.L. PARKER

Transportation Captain.................................CINDY PARKER

Production Assistants..................................JAMES LaCLAIR
                                                 SEAN SWINT
                                                 JONATHAN WATSON
                                                 STROKE T. RENIGADE
                                                 BOWEN ASTROP

Greensperson...JEANNE M. HALL

189

Craft Service...TRICIA SAMMONS

Police Coordinator..MIKE SMITH

Playback Operator...GREG MORSE

Scenic billboards by.......................................TOM S. GUNTER

Catering..........................LOCATION CATERING OF THE SOUTH, INC.

Negative Cutter.............................D. BASSETT & ASSOCIATES

Color Timers..BOB PUTYNKOWSKI
                                                            TOM SHAFFER

Titles & Optical Effects..................................PACIFIC TITLE

Processing by.......................CINEFILM LABORATORY, INC., ATLANTA

Special Visual Effects by..............INTROVISION INTERNATIONAL, INC.

Sound Re-recording by.......................................JDH SOUND

Sound Services provided by........................SPROCKET SYSTEMS,
                                            A DIVISION OF LUCASFILM LTD.

Supervising Sound Editor........................GLORIA S. BORDERS

Dialogue Editors.......................................RONALD JACOBS
                                                        MELISSA DIETZ

ADR Editor..TOM BELLFORT

Effects Editor..TIM HOLLAND

Foley Editor..SANDINA BAILO-LAPE

Assistant Editors.......................................KAREN HARDING
                                                        CLARE FREEMAN

Foley Artist..ROBIN HARLAN

Foley Recordist...DAVID SLUSSER

Our gratitude to:

Factory location...Fulton Supply Company, Atlanta, Georgia
Darlin's Restaurant
Outdoor Today Inc.
Irving Vendig, Creator-Writer, "The Edge of Night"

THE CAST

Hoke Colburn..MORGAN FREEMAN

Daisy Werthan..JESSICA TANDY

Boolie Werthan...DAN AYKROYD

Florine Werthan..PATTI LUPONE

Idella...ESTHER ROLLE

Miss McClatchey..JOANN HAVRILLA

Oscar...WILLIAM HALL, JR.

Dr. Weil..ALVIN M. SUGARMAN

Nonie..CLARICE F. GEIGERMAN

Miriam..MURIEL MOORE

Beulah..SYLVIA KALER

Neighbor Lady...CAROLYN GOLD

Katie Bell..CRYSTAL R. FOX

Red Mitchell..BOB HANNAH

Trooper #1...RAY McKINNON

Trooper #2...ASHLEY JOSEY

Slick..JACK ROUSSO

Insurance Agent..FRED FASER

Soloist..INDRA A. THOMAS

Stunt Double...DANNY MABRY

Additional Voices......................................ROYCE APPLEGATE
                                                       JUNE CHRISTOPHER
                                                       LEIGH FRENCH
                                                       ARCHIE HAHN
                                                       EUGENE LEE
                                                       FELTON PERRY
                                                       RUTH SILVEIRA
                                                       GREGORY SNEGOFF
                                                       LYNNE STEWART
                                                       ARNOLD TURNER

Stand-ins...................................LETHA PERKINS, LEON WATKINS,
                                            B.J. HUGHES, COLLEEN HESS,
                                            LOIS MIDDLEBROOKS

"Driving Miss Daisy" was first produced Off-Broadway by
Playwrights Horizons, New York City in 1987.
It was subsequently produced by the Daisy Company in association
with Playwrights Horizon Off-Broadway in 1987.

THE MUSIC

"AFTER THE BALL"
Words and Music by Charles K. Harris
Published by Charles K. Harris Publishing Company, Inc.

"I LOVE YOU (FOR SENTIMENTAL REASONS)"
Written by Deek Watson and Derek Best
Performed by Ella Fitzgerald
Courtesy of MCA Records

"JINGLE BELLS"
Arranged and Performed by Les Peel
Courtesy of Capitol Production Music/Ole Georg

"KISS OF FIRE"
Written by Lester Allen and Robert Hill
Performed by Louis Armstrong
Courtesy of MCA Records

"SANTA BABY"
Written by Tony Springer, Phil Spring and Joann Jarvitz
Performed by Eartha Kitt
Courtesy of RCA Records

"SONG TO THE MOON" (excerpt from the opera "Rusalka")
Composed by Antonin Dvorak
Performed by Gabriela Benackova & the Czech Philharmonic
Courtesy of Supraphon Int'l

"WHAT A FRIEND WE HAVE IN JESUS"
Sung by Little Friendship Missionary Baptist Church Choir,
Decatur, Georgia
Indra A. Thomas, soloist

Original soundtrack album on
VARESÉ SARABANDE
CD's and cassettes

Lenses and PANAGLIDE (R) Camera by PANAVISION (R)

Prints by TECHNICOLOR (R)

DOLBY STEREO (R) (LOGO)
in selected theatres

This motion picture
(c) 1989 Warner Bros. Inc.
Screenplay
(c) 1989 Warner Bros. Inc.
All original music compositions
(c) 1989 Warner-Tamerlane Publishing Corp.

THE ZANUCK COMPANY (logo)

Distributed by Warner Bros. (logo)
A Warner Communications Company

MPAA RATED "PG"

Used with permission of Warner Bros. Inc.

11

MISCELLANEOUS

There are certain basic press releases that we prepare separately or as part of our press kits: announcement stories, follow-up stories, start and end of production stories, casting announcements, news releases, biographies, feature stories, credits, fact sheets, items, storylines, and format stories, among others.

But there are also others that are not part of the publicity routine. They are special stories created for special needs. Sometimes they are in response to a problem that has arisen. At other times they are backgrounder pieces that provide useful information.

The point is, the publicist should always be on the lookout for what might prove useful in the way of press handouts, over and above the customary. Sometimes all you need to do is ask yourself, "If I were the media, what additional information would be useful to me?" If you can think of something, provide it. Or, look at anything that comes to your attention and see how it might benefit your show or your client. Are you publicizing a rerun of a TV movie? What did the reviewers say the first time around? If the show got good reviews, now's the time to use excerpts. Was the movie one of the top-rated shows of the season or of all time? Now's the time to use that information (or to recycle it, if you used it as a follow-up story after the show aired initially).

Let's look at some releases that served a valuable, special purpose.

Emmy Awards Follow-up   Viewers who watched the 1991 Primetime Emmy Awards noticed that quite a number of the stars were wearing red ribbons. Weissman/Angellotti, the PR agency representing the Academy of Television Arts & Sciences, found out what the story was behind the red ribbons and sent out a two-page news release.

This was good journalism, because in gathering this information, they were able to provide inquiring reporters, and curious viewers, with the information they needed.

It was also good public relations. Since the story was sent out after the Emmy Awards telecast, it obviously could not benefit the program any more by attracting more viewers. But the story benefited the TV Academy by providing the information as a public service, and it created good will between the TV Academy and the individuals involved with this red ribbon demonstration of support on behalf of people living with AIDS. Such releases need careful wording. Notice the third paragraph, in particular.

"The Simpsons"   That same year, the TV Academy came under
Q&A   considerable criticism for the way its awards nominations
                       were structured. Why were "The Simpsons" placed in the
animation category rather than the comedy series category?   Why was "The
Civil War" placed in a category where it competed against "Unsolved
Mysteries" and "Entertainment Tonight?" And other questions.

One TV writer after another kept raising these questions. So the PR agency prepared a position paper, stating each question and providing the Academy's answer to that question. This three-page Q&A piece was then sent out to the media and others concerned with these issues.

This is a good way of handling a controversial situation. You don't want to run away from it, and you can't run away from it. You must deal with it directly. By spelling out the issues and providing written answers, there's less chance of misunderstanding and misinterpretation. Also, by making this information available to everyone at once, there's a better chance that the media will deal with the matter and then go on to something else, rather than keep dragging it out from one writer to the next and from one broadcast to another. If you can influence opinion to your way of thinking, great. But if not, you and your client can feel at least that you gave it your best shot and that, hopefully, you got a fair hearing.

"LifeStories"   Sometimes a show or TV series requires a backgrounder
Backgrounder   piece. Such was the case with NBC-TV's innovative,
                      one-hour anthology, "LifeStories," which explored crucial
health issues in a dramatic, entertaining and informative way.

The series dealt with such issues as colon cancer, in-utero surgery, heart disease, alcoholism, cosmetic surgery, Alzheimer's disease, aplastic anemia and bone marrow transplants.

To help the media write and talk about this series, Mahoney Communications, Inc., which prepared the press kit and represented the series for Orion Television Entertainment, prepared a backgrounder, providing some dramatic facts and figures about the various issues. The excellent, six-page informational "feature" was titled:

CUTTING EDGE HEALTH ISSUES UNVEILED IN 'LIFESTORIES'

Endorsements   "LifeStories," which sought to spread the word on
                     preventive health care to the public, received much praise
from various organizations. Sometimes these endorsements come of their
own accord. At other times you (or your client) may ask for comment and,

hopefully, a statement of support. When that happens, call it to the attention of the media and the public. Such endorsements may be sent out as a separate news release or made part of your press kit.

"The Sun Sometimes a special fact sheet can be very useful. Take the case
Also Rises" of "The Sun Also Rises." You may know or find out that this is
Chronology not the first thing by Ernest Hemingway to be adapted to
television. For that matter, some of his works were also made into theatrical motion pictures. You can be sure that the media will raise these questions. "Who was in 'For Whom the Bell Tolls?' When did that air? Was 'Farewell to Arms' a feature film or a TV show, or both? Who was in it..." and on and on and on.

So, anticipate these questions. Get ahead of the game. Find the answers. Organize them for easy reference. Do the work when you have the time, before you get bombarded with media phone calls and you have to scramble for the information.

See the chronological way the network handled this information, splitting it up into two sections: <u>Hemingway on Television</u> and <u>Hemingway on the Screen</u>.

WEISSMAN / ANGELLOTTI

3855 Lankershim Boulevard • North Hollywood, California 91614 • (818) 763-2975 • FAX (818) 760-4847

NEWS

PRESS CONTACTS;
  WEISSMAN/ANGELLOTTI
  Murray Weissman
  Mark Rosch
  818/763-2975

WHAT'S THE STORY BEHIND ALL THOSE STARS WEARING RED RIBBONS ON THE PRIMETIME EMMY TELECAST?

NORTH HOLLYWOOD, CA., Aug. 28--Why were more than 80 stars on last Sunday's (8/25) Primetime Emmy Awards telecast wearing red ribbons and who are the two people most responsible for it?

The Ribbon Project, a movement of Visual AIDS Artists" Caucus, is to demonstrate compassion for people living with AIDS and gainsupport for research and trreatment of the disease.

The actors wearing red ribbons on the Emmy telecast were approached to cooperate in advance of the show by David Michaels, a member of the Academy of Television Arts & Sciences Board of Govermnors (Daytime Programming Branch) and producer of "The $100,000 Pyramid," and Susan A. Simons, an officer of the Academy and a program development executive with Kelly Entertainment. Their action was totally an independent action, and did not represent an endorsement by the Academy or Fox.

Prior to the telecast Michaels and Simons sent explanatory letters about the project to all Emmy presenters and nominees suggesting they help AIDS awareness by wearing red ribbons. Co-host Jamie Lee Curtis told the television audience why her fellow actors were wearing ribbons. Among stars wearing ribbons on Emmy night were Bea Arthur, Corbin Bernson, Delta Burke,

(more)

198

Carol Burnett, Dixie Carter, Ted Danson, Dom DeLuise, Charles Durning, Richard Dysart, Peter Falk, Faith Ford, Estelle Getty, John Glover, John Goodman, Harry Hamlin, Dennis Hopper, James Earl Jones, Carol Kane, Sam Kinison, Angela Lansbury, Richard Lewis, Marlee Matlin, Mike Myers, Dennis Miller, Richard Mulligan, Craig T. Nelson, Merlin Olsen, Park Overall, Rhea Perlman, Luke Perry, Annie Potts, Burt Reynolds, Doris Roberts, Susan Ruttan, Bob Saget, Jimmy Smits, Alan Thicke, Marlo Thomas, Michael Tucker, Betty White and Robert Wuhl.

The Ribbon Project kicked off June 2 on the Tony Awards telecast with some of the following winners and presenters wearing red ribbons: Jeremy Irons, Tyne Daly, Topol, Julie Harris, Lea Salonga, Jonathamn Pryce and Stockard Channing.

Michaels and Simons, who also co-chair the Academy's Daytime Emmy Show and Awards Committee and serve as West Coast Chairs of The Ribbon Project, moved the practise into further national attention by placing ribbons on 19 stars during the Daytime Emmy telecast on CBS on June 26. On that show Ed Asner notified the audience about the significance of the ribbons.

Said Michaels and Simons:

"When you think of the millions of homes tuned in to watch Primetime and Daytime Emmy and theTonys you have a measure of our satisfaction in pinning those ribbons on all those lapels. The Ribbon Project is something we're dedicated to keep doing with determination. . .since it helps to raise the consciousness level of an entire nation to one of the most awesome problems of our time--AIDS."

#

N E W S
IMMEDIATE
RELEASE

43RD ANNUAL PRIMETIME EMMY AWARDS

ACADEMY OF
TELEVISION
ARTS & SCIENCES

5220 LANKERSHIM BLVD.
NORTH HOLLYWOOD
CALIFORNIA 91601-3109
TEL (818) 754-2800
FAX (818) 761-ATAS

OFFICIAL ACADEMY ANSWERS TO QUESTIONS POSED ABOUT THE 43RD ANNUAL EMMY AWARDS NOMINATIONS

July 24, 1991

TO: Media and Others Concerned
FROM: John Leverence, Awards Director
Academy of Television Arts & Sciences

1. Why is "The Simpsons" placed in the animation rather than the comedy series category?

The Emmy Awards makes distinctions about programming in order to classify it into competitive categories. A primary distinction is between the mediums of animation and live action. Any program that is more than 65% animation is considered an animated program and must enter in the animation category. The Awards Committee invited representatives from "The Simpsons" to argue the case for moving it from animation to comedy series. Representatives were expected to attend the meeting, but they cancelled at the last minute, and the matter never made it from the agenda to the table.

2. Why are the writers of "The Simpsons" not allowed to enter in the comedy series writing category?

Several years ago the Board of Governors accepted the animators' argument that animation writing, directing and producing were so intertwined and inseparable, that all three should be judged together.

-more-

3.   Why isn't "The Simpsons" on the Fox telecast?

Animation is not a televised category. The Board of Governors recognizes that there are already too many categories on the telecast, and it does not want to add any more. In fact, this year it reduced the number by two categories. And while fans of "The Simpsons" might make some good arguments for including its category on the telecast, fans of cultural and informational programming can make equally good arguments for the classical and informational categories, which are both off-air

4.   Why are the guest performer categories off-air?

When the guest performer categories were originated several years ago, there were two categories (one for comedy series and one for drama series). They were on-air for two years, and when they were expanded to four categories, they were on-air for yet another year. Four years ago, the Board of Governors sought to reduce the number of on-air categories in order to give the telecast producer a better opportunity to do more than hand out awards. Since at that time there were 17 performer categories - many more than any other type of on-air category - it was decided to move the four guest performer categories.

The Academy does not make a value distinction between an Emmy given at the Creative Arts Awards or the telecast. When peers recognize excellence in the work of peers, the forum is irrelevant to the honor.

5.   Why are there only four nominees in the drama series lead actress category?

It is generally intended to have five nominees per category. From time to time there will be a tie for fifth place, and the Awards Committee is asked to designate either the higher or lower number of nominations. In this instance, as in numerous other instances in this and other Emmys, the committee chose the lesser number. The

-more-

decision was based on the "hourglass" shape of the stack of anonymous percentages provided by the accountants: the top of the hourglass contained the four top vote-getters, then there was a distinct reduction in the votes for each entrant, and then there were the rest of the entrants, making up the lower half of the hourglass. Had the top of the hourglass contained six top vote-getters, then the committee would have gone with all six.

6. Why did "The Civil War" get only two nominations?

The Emmy Awards is a voluntary competition in which individuals who are eligible in any given category have the right to enter. Only two entries were made. Both entries were nominated. A dozen or more entries could have been made, but they were not.

7. Why is "The Civil War" placed in a category where it is competing against "Unsolved Mysteries" and "Entertainment Tonight"?

The general rule in the Emmy competition is that nominations in a category compete against one another, and the one with the highest score takes the Emmy. The general rule does not apply in this case. Informational series (and specials) nominations do not compete against one another. Each is judged on its own terms and given a separate score. Any nomination in informational series (or specials) that receives 2/3 approval of the panelists receives an Emmy, and so there is the possibility of one, more than one or no winner.

8. Why is "The Kennedy Center Honors" placed in a category where it is competing against "In Living Color" and "The Muppets Celebrate Jim Henson"?

Much like informational series (noted above), variety-music-comedy programming is judged non-competitively. After each nomination is judged on its own terms and given its separate score, the nomination with the highest score wins the sole Emmy given in this category.

-end-

FEATURE STORY

CUTTING EDGE HEALTH ISSUES UNVEILED IN "LIFESTORIES"

LOS ANGELES -- NBC's innovative one-hour anthology, "LifeStories," explores crucial health issues in a dramatic, entertaining and informative context. Portraying critical issues through humanistic values, "LifeStories" ultimately hopes to save viewers' lives by making them aware of the importance of proper and preventive health care.

The series examines clinical and psychological aspects of each week's different topic, some of which are life-threatening, others which exact an emotional price on the patient and family members. Each topic is extremely timely -- as each has the potential to affect every American's life.

COLON CANCER

In the pilot episode, "LifeStories" depicts a healthy, middle-aged man who, after an annual physical, discovers he has colon cancer.

o   This year, 110,000 new cases of colon cancer will be reported in the United States. An estimated 53,000 patients will die from it.

o   More common in men, and often thought of as the "hidden" cancer, this disease can be detected through standard tests included in a complete physical.

(more)

203

ORION
TELEVISION ENTERTAINMENT

1888 Century Park East. 6th Floor, Los Angeles, CA 90067 (213) 282-0550

Colon Cancer - continued

o   People at risk are:

        -       Those with a family history of polyps (benign growths
                arising from a mucous membrane) in the colon or
                rectum.

        -       Individuals with inflammatory bowel disease.

        -       Those who have a high fat and/or low fiber diet.

IN-UTERO SURGERY

This fascinating surgery is performed in "LifeStories" on the
fetus of a couple in their late 30s, who have experienced great
difficulty in conceiving.

o   Recently approved by the Food and Drug Administration in
        June, 1990, in-utero is the newest technology in pre-natal
        surgery.

o   Through an incision in the mother's stomach and uterus
        (similar to that of a cesarean section), the growing fetus
        can be extracted and surgery performed to correct
        abnormalities discovered through ultrasound. Once surgery
        is complete, the fetus is placed back in the womb, to
        continue healthy development.

(more)

HEART DISEASE

"LifeStories" will capture the tense drama of what occurs in the body during the first 47 minutes of a heart attack, measured in real time.

o   One out of two individuals in the United States die from heart or blood vessel disease (including failure, defects, strokes, etc.) every year. 513,700 die specifically from heart attacks. (Source: American Heart Association)

o   Men under age 65 are at greater risk of having a heart attack. Yet, over the age of 65, both sexes are at equal risk.

o   Family history, cigarette smoking, high blood pressure, high blood cholesterol and obesity are all contributing factors to heart disease.

ALCOHOLISM

o   "LifeStories" portrays the intervention method through a family who confronts an alcoholic member, much to her surprise, as a last-ditch effort to save her life.

o   Over 17.7 million Americans suffer from alcoholism, a disease which contributes to 97,500 deaths annually. Countless other lives are destroyed through alcohol's devastating effects.

(more)

Alcoholism - continued

o   Addressing one of the most difficult aspects of recovery,
     getting the alcoholic to recognize their problem, the
     "intervention method" attempts to call the alcoholic's
     attention to the problem by family members simultaneously
     confronting the alcoholic and describing how the disease
     is affecting the family.

o   The final step is to enroll in a recovery program, to
     begin a life of sobriety.

COSMETIC SURGERY

As four people sit in a plastic surgeon's waiting room,
"LifeStories" explores the emotional facets of cosmetic surgery.
The episode explores how each character arrived at this point in
their life, and how the procedures performed on them will change
-- or fail to change -- their lives.

o   Approximately 600,000 aesthetic surgical procedures are
     performed annually in the United States. Many are purely
     cosmetic; others, a necessary reconstruction.

o   The psychological aspects are great for those who choose a
     permanent, surgical procedure to enhance or improve their
     physical appearance.

(more)

APLASTIC ANEMIA AND BONE MARROW TRANSPLANTS

"LifeStories" brings an emotional drama to life as a couple searches for the child they gave up for adoption several years earlier, in order to find a bone marrow donor for their younger child, afflicted with aplastic anemia, who will die without a bone marrow transplant.

o   Aplastic anemia is a rare (five cases per million population) but extremely serious disorder that results from the unexplained failure of the bone marrow to produce blood cells.

o   One of the two major treatment options is bone marrow transplantation, which is the recommended procedure for patients under 25 years of age.

o   Recently, people not related to the patient have been able to donate their bone marrow, however, the chances of finding a match is one in 20,000.

(more)

ALZHEIMER'S DISEASE

o   Alzheimer's disease, a progressive, degenerative disease that attacks the brain, impairing memory, thought processes and behavior, currently afflicts more than four million Americans.

o   Alzheimer's disease is the fourth leading cause of death among adults, claiming over 100,000 lives annually.

o   Currently, there is no cure for Alzheimer's, and if no means of prevention are discovered, an estimated 12 to 14 million Americans will be affected by the year 2040.

In addition to the topics previously described, "LifeStories" will address near-death experiences, the physiology of love and desire, psychopathic personalities, gunshot trauma, and spontaneous recovery from fatal diseases.

"LifeStories" is a production of Ohlmeyer Communications in association with Jeffrey Lewis Productions and Orion Television Entertainment.

= = =

CONTACT: MAHONEY COMMUNICATIONS, INC.
             Barbara Bishop/Stacy Cafagna
             Trisha Cardoso Bouali
             (213) 550-3922

LIFESTORIES

NATIONAL MEDICAL ORGANIZATION ACKNOWLEDGEMENTS

National medical organizations, quick to realize the unique and extraordinary vehicle "LifeStories" provides for spreading the word on preventive health care to the public, are rallying in support of the series. The following organizations have provided the series with written acknowledgements:

THE AMERICAN CANCER SOCIETY

"The American Cancer Society applauds NBC's efforts to reach viewers nationwide with information about cancer prevention, early detection and treatment through programs such as 'LifeStories.' We realize that the entertainment medium is an excellent way for people to receive and respond to health messages which can change their behavior and ultimately, perhaps, even save their lives."

Robert J. Schweitzer, M.D.
President, American Cancer Society

(more)

1888 Century Park East, 6th Floor, Los Angeles, CA 90067 (213) 282-0550

AMERICAN HEALTH FOUNDATION

"Television has the power not only to entertain millions of people each day, it also has the power to educate and inform. That is why a series such as 'LifeStories' can be of interest to all of us -- laymen and medical professionals."

The medical profession has always stressed that awareness and educating the public are vital tools not only in treating diseases, but also in their prevention. With a program such as "LifeStories," prevention should become a national priority."

Dr. E.L. Wynder
American Health Foundation

SURGEON GENERAL OF THE UNITED STATES:

"So many diseases are preventable, and each of us needs to consider the short and long-range consequences of these choices-- consequences for the individual, the family and the country. I join in calling for a "culture of character" in which our citizens enhance their freedom, independence and dignity by embracing good health care practices and changing those behaviors which place them at risk."

Dr. Antonia C. Novella
Surgeon General of the United States

= = =

HEMINGWAY ON TELEVISION

1984	THE SUN ALSO RISES (NBC miniseries) starring Jane Seymour, Hart Bochner, Leonard Nimoy, Robert Carradine, Zeljko Ivanec, Ian Charleson and Stephane Audran directed by James Goldstone
1981	THE BEST OF FRIENDS (adapted from "Three Day Blow" and presented on "Liberty Mutual")
1979	MY OLD MAN (CBS movie) starring Kristy McNichol directed by John Erman
1978	SOLDIER'S HOME (presented on "The American Short Story") starring Richard Backus directed by Robert Young
1959/ 1960	Series of four "CBS Specials" directed by John Frankenheimer: THE KILLERS THE FIFTH COLUMN THE SNOWS OF KILIMANJARO FIFTH COLUMN
1959	FOR WHOM THE BELL TOLLS (presented on "Playhouse 90") starring Maria Schell, Jason Robards, Jr., and Maureen Stapleton directed by John Frankenheimer
1958	FIFTY GRAND (presented on "Kraft Television Theatre") starring Ralph Meeker
1957	TO HAVE AND HAVE NOT (presented on "Lux Video Theatre") starring Edmond O'Brien
	THE WORLD OF NICK ADAMS (presented on "Seven Lively Arts") starring Eli Wallach, William Marshall and Steven Hill directed by Robert Mulligan
1955	A FAREWELL TO ARMS (presented on "Climax") starring Guy Madison and Diana Lynn
1954	THE GAMBLER, THE NUN AND THE RADIO (presented on "Omnibus") starring Geraldine Fitzgerald and Harry Townes
	THE BATTLER (presented on "Playwrights '56") starring Paul Newman and Phyllis Kirk
1953	THE BATTLER (presented on "Omnibus") starring Jack Palance and Chester Morris
	THE CAPITOL OF THE WORLD (ballet presented on "Omnibus")

211

(more)

HEMINGWAY ON THE SCREEN

1977   ISLANDS IN THE STREAM
starring George C. Scott, Claire Bloom and Hart Bochner
directed by Franklin J. Schaffner

1964   THE KILLERS
starring Lee Marvin
directed by Don Siegel

1962   HEMINGWAY'S ADVENTURES OF A YOUNG MAN
starring Richard Beymer and Paul Newman
directed by Martin Ritt

1958   THE OLD MAN AND THE SEA
starring Spencer Tracy
directed by John Sturges

1958   THE GUN RUNNERS (adapted from "To Have and Have Not")
starring Audie Murphy and Eddie Albert
directed by Don Siegel

1957   THE SUN ALSO RISES
starring Tyrone Power, Ava Gardner, Errol Flynn, Eddie Albert, Mel
Ferrer, Juliette Greco and Robert Evans
directed by Henry King

           A FAREWELL TO ARMS
starring Rock Hudson and Jennifer Jones
directed by Charles Vidor

1952   THE SNOWS OF KILIMANJARO
starring Gregory Peck, Ava Gardner, and Susan Hayward
directed by Henry King

1950   UNDER MY SKIN (adapted from "My Old Man")
starring John Garfield and Micheline Presle
directed by Jean Negulesco

           THE BREAKING POINT (adapted from "To Have and Have Not")
starring John Garfield and Patricia Neal
directed by Michael Curtiz

1947   THE MACOMBER AFFAIR
starring Gregory Peck and Joan Bennett
directed by Zoltan Korda

1946   THE KILLERS
starring Burt Lancaster and Ava Gardner
directed by Robert Siodmak

(more)

1944   TO HAVE AND HAVE NOT
        starring Humphrey Bogart and Lauren Bacall
        directed by Howard Hawks

1943   FOR WHOM THE BELL TOLLS
        starring Gary Cooper and Ingrid Bergman
        directed by Sam Wood

1937   SPANISH EARTH
        directed by Joris Ivens

1932   · A FAREWELL TO ARMS
        starring Gary Cooper and Helen Hayes
        directed by Frank Borzage

————o————

November, 1984
#1189Y

## 12

Reference Sources

REFERENCE GUIDES

THE COMPLETE DIRECTORY TO PRIME TIME NETWORK TV SHOWS
1946 - PRESENT
Tim Brooks, Earle Marsh
Ballantine Books

THE FILM ENCYCLOPEDIA
The Most Comprehensive Encyclopedia of World Cinema in a Single
Volume
A Perigee Book
(Good for mini-bios of movie people; check date of publication; may need to
update credits)

LEONARD MALTIN'S TV MOVIES AND VIDEO GUIDE
A Signet Book/New American Library
Updated regularly
Titles, stars, production staff, storyline, evaluation

THE WORLD ALMANAC & BOOK OF FACTS
Copyright Newspaper Enterprise Association
Scripps-Howard, issued annually

WRITING, GRAMMAR, RULES, PUNCTUATION
HARBRACE COLLEGE HANDBOOK
John C. Hodges, Mary E. Whitten
Harcourt Brace Jovanovich, Inc.
(get ninth edition or later)
Excellent book on style, punctuation, writing rules; easy reference

THE ELEMENTS OF STYLE
William Strunk, Jr.
The Macmillan Company
Classic and definitive

JOURNALISTIC STYLE
MANUAL OF STYLE & USAGE
The New York Times/Times Books

AP STYLEBOOK
AP NewsFeature
50 Rockefeller Plaza
New York, NY 10020
212/621-1821 $9.75 plus $2.50 mailing (1991)

ORGANIZATIONS

Directors Guild of America
213/289-2000

Publicists Guild of America
13949 Ventura Blvd. Ste. 302
Sherman Oaks, CA 91423
Local 818 (IATSE)
818/905-1541

Producers Guild of America
310/557-0807

Screen Actors Guild
213/465-4600
(for locating actors' agents)

Writers Guild of America, West
310/550-1000

ACADEMY OF MOTION PICTURE ARTS & SCIENCES
8949 Wilshire Blvd.
—BH 90211-1972

(Academy Library)
333 S. La Cienega Blvd.
310/247-3020
(good library; can also get phone info.)

ACADEMY OF TELEVISION ARTS & SCIENCES
5220 Lankershim Blvd.
No. Hollywood, CA 91601
818/754-2800
reference library located at
3500 W. Olive Ave. #700
Burbank, CA 91505
818/953-7575 (can get info by phone)

$19.95

<u>Also available:</u>

PUBLICITY ADVICE & HOW-TO HANDBOOK by Rolf Gompertz

This is an advice and how-to book for any area of public relations. It is a reference manual for PR practitioners and those entering this profession. It may be used as a practical training manual by PR departments and PR agencies. The manual serves as a text book for the author's course, "Elements of Publicity," which he teaches at UCLA Extension. It is also used by other instructors.

The book deals with such matters as structuring and writing the pitch letter, news release, fact sheet, biography, feature story, items and captions.

It explains how to deal with print and broadcast media, how to handle events, press events and press conferences. There is a useful chapter on photos, captions, and photo coverage. The book provides information about clipping and monitoring services and various distribution methods.

The book contains practical information on video news releases (VNRs), electronic press kits (EPKs), satellite media tours, and satellite distribution.

A final chapter deals with jobs, salaries and job hunting.

Anonymous student evaluations of the course and the book elicited the following comments:

> *"Your book has become my 'bible' of Public Relations."*
> *"An excellent reference tool which can be used on all levels of professional PR endeavor."*
> *"Very, very clear....Easy to read...A great source of information."*
> *"The text really helped me a lot and covered everything I needed to know. Very informative, easy to read and good examples."*
> *"Well done and beneficial, both for course work and every-day on-the-job assignments."*

Gompertz is a public relations veteran, independent consultant, and writer. He spent 30 years on staff in the Media Relations Department of NBC, serving as Director, General Programs from 1983-1987. He then formed his own company, Rolf Gompertz Communications, offering writing services and PR consulting in entertainment areas and non-entertainment areas, covering products, issues and services.

The handbook is 8 1/2 x 11, with sample press releases appearing actual size.

ISBN No. 0-918248-07-8   Library of Congress Catalog Card No. 88-50026

<u>Publisher:</u>
The Word Doctor Publications
P.O. Box 9761
No. Hollywood, CA 91609-1761
Phone: 818/980-3576
FAX: 818/985-7922